PENGUIN BOOK

LITERATURE AND C

The author of *Literature and Criticism* was a Gloucestershire man who was educated at Tewkesbury and Cambridge. After a decade's schoolteaching in the industrial Midlands, he did extra-mural and W.E.A. lecturing in his own county for several years. He wrote books on Edward Thomas and T. F. Powys. H. Coombes died in 1980.

BB 0140 136924 1002

Leabharlanna Atha Cliath
PEMBROKE LIBRARY
Inv/93 : 1404   Price IR£6.15
Title: LITERATURE AND CRITIC
Class: 801.95

SANTRY BOOKSTORE
DUBLIN CORPORATION PUBLIC LIBRARIES

H. COOMBES

LITERATURE AND CRITICISM

Discussion, suggestion, formulation,
are fertilizing when they are frank and sincere....
Be generous and delicate and pursue the prize.
HENRY JAMES

SANTRY BOOKSTORE
DUBLIN CORPORATION PUBLIC LIBRARIES

PENGUIN BOOKS
IN ASSOCIATION WITH CHATTO & WINDUS

PENGUIN BOOKS

Published by the Penguin Group
Penguin Books Ltd, 27 Wrights Lane, London W8 5TZ, England
Penguin Books USA Inc., 375 Hudson Street, New York, New York 10014, USA
Penguin Books Australia Ltd, Ringwood, Victoria, Australia
Penguin Books Canada Ltd, 10 Alcorn Avenue, Toronto, Ontario, Canada M4V 3B2
Penguin Books (NZ) Ltd, 182–190 Wairau Road, Auckland 10, New Zealand

Penguin Books Ltd, Registered Offices: Harmondsworth, Middlesex, England

First published by Chatto & Windus 1953
Published in Pelican Books 1963
Reprinted in Penguin Books 1991
1 3 5 7 9 10 8 6 4 2

Copyright 1953 by H. Coombes
All rights reserved

Printed in England by Clays Ltd, St Ives plc
Set in Monotype Baskerville

Except in the United States of America, this book is sold subject
to the condition that it shall not, by way of trade or otherwise, be lent,
re-sold, hired out, or otherwise circulated without the publisher's
prior consent in any form of binding or cover other than that in
which it is published and without a similar condition including this
condition being imposed on the subsequent purchaser

CONTENTS

ACKNOWLEDGEMENTS

My thanks are due to Messrs Constable and Co. Ltd for their kind permission to use the passage by George Meredith; to Mr T. S. Eliot and to Messrs Faber and Faber Ltd for passages from *The Collected Poems of T. S. Eliot 1909–1935* and from *Four Quartets*; to Mrs Frieda Lawrence and Messrs William Heinemann Ltd for the D. H. Lawrence passages, and to the same publishers for the extract from *Swinburne's Collected Poetical Works*; to Dr F. R. Leavis and Messrs Chatto and Windus for the passage, on page *9* from *The Common Pursuit*, and to the same publishers for the two poems from *The Collected Poems of Isaac Rosenberg*; to the Oxford University Press for the poem and extracts from *Poems of Gerard Manley Hopkins* and *Gerard Manley Hopkins*, by G. F. Lahey, s.j.; to Mrs Helen Thomas and Messrs Faber and Faber Ltd for the poem from *The Collected Poems of Edward Thomas*; to Mrs W. B. Yeats and Messrs Macmillan and Co. Ltd for the poem and extract from *The Collected Poems of W. B. Yeats*, and to the same publishers, by permission of the Trustees of the Hardy Estate, for the two poems from *The Collected Poems of Thomas Hardy*.

H.C.

INTRODUCTORY NOTE

BROADLY speaking, we can say that a good literary critic, when he is practising his 'art' – that is to say, when he is committing his criticism to paper – is characteristically engaged in doing two things, or one of two things: he gives us, as completely and as clearly as he can, his considered response to a writer, to a play, a novel, a poem, an essay, and so can help us to a fuller enjoyment and understanding of the experience in and behind the writing; or he reveals, by examining a piece of writing in detail, the elements in the writing which combine to make its particular quality. In practice, of course, these two activities usually go together: a good critic, knowing that his account and evaluation of an author must depend on the actual words written by the author, supports his fundamental remarks and judgements with pieces (however slight) of examined text, the text out of which his judgements rise. When we come across a hazy account, in general terms, of an author or of a piece of writing, we may conclude that a mediocre critic is at work, and that he is probably approaching his author with some degree of predisposition, perhaps with some admixture of prejudice or favouritism. Very often such a critic would give himself away if forced to analyse his author in detail. The fact that his favouritism or prejudice may be unconscious does not excuse his lack of critical discipline. A critic should be as fully conscious as possible of what he is doing.

The validity of this little book depends upon the belief that the character of a writer's whole achievement can only be felt and assessed by responding sensitively to the way in which he uses words, and that the capacity to make such a response can be formed or greatly enhanced by a training in literary criticism.

D. H. Lawrence says some excellent things about critics and criticism:

Literary criticism can be no more than a reasoned account of the feeling produced upon the critic by the book he is criticizing. Criticism can never be a science: it is, in the first place, much too personal, and in the second, it is concerned with values that science ignores. The touch-stone is emotion, not reason. We judge a work of art by its effect on our sincere and vital emotion, and nothing else. All the critical twiddle-twaddle about style and form, all this pseudo-scientific classifying and analysing of books in an imitation-botanical fashion, is mere impertinence and most dull jargon.

A critic must be able to *feel* the impact of a work of art in all its complexity and its force. To do so, he must be a man of force and complexity himself, which few critics are. A man with a paltry, impudent nature will never write anything but paltry, impudent criticism. And a man who is *emotionally* educated is rare as a phoenix. The more scholastically educated a man is generally, the more he is an emotional boor.

More than this, even an artistically and emotionally educated man must be a man of good faith. He must have the courage to admit what he feels, as well as the flexibility to *know* what he feels. So Sainte-Beuve remains, to me, a great critic. And a man like Macaulay, brilliant as he is, is unsatisfactory, because he is not honest. He is emotionally very alive, but he juggles his feelings. He prefers a fine effect to the sincere statement of his aesthetic and emotional reaction. He is quite intellectually capable of giving us a true account of what he feels. But not morally. A critic must be emotionally alive in every fibre, intellectually capable and skilful in essential logic, and then morally very honest.

These statements of Lawrence are not given here for simple and wholesale swallowing. For instance, we must be sure we know what he intends when he 'opposes' reason to emotion, and what he means by 'essential logic'. But the passage will be found to bear much pondering, and it raises radical issues with the insight and strength and certitude that belong to a fine critic.

Side by side with it we may consider the following paragraph by F. R. Leavis (he is discussing an American critic's belief that the intention of Henry James in his novels was closely bound up with a certain philosophical system, that in fact the writing of the novels depended largely on the author's having adopted that system):

But what I have to insist on is that intention in the important sense can only be determined by the tests applied in literary criticism. The analysis and judgement of works of literary art belong to the literary critic, who *is* one in so far as he observes a disciplined relevance in response, comment and determination of significance. He is concerned with the work in front of him as something that should contain within itself the reason why it is so and not otherwise. The more experience – experience of life and literature together – he brings to bear on it the better, of course; and it is true that extraneous information may make him more percipient. But the business of critical intelligence will remain what it was: to ensure relevance of response and to determine what is actually *there* in the work of art. The critic will be especially wary how he uses extraneous knowledge about the writer's intentions. Intentions are nothing in art except as realized, and the tests of realization will remain what they were. They are applied in the operation of the critic's sensibility; they are a matter of his sense, derived from his literary experience, of what the living thing feels like – of the difference between that which has been willed and put there, or represents no profound integration, and that which grows from a deep centre of life. These tests may very well reveal that the deep animating intention (if that is the right word) is something very different from the intention the author would declare.

As with the Lawrence passage there are things here which should be clarified by further discussion but which are outside our range of the moment: 'profound integration', for example. But the gist of the passage, namely the emphasis put on the necessity for the critic of attending firmly to the 'work in front of him', is forcefully clear, and what the paragraph says is relevant to the purpose of this book, making due allowance for the more elementary nature of such a book.

Now Lawrence is a great creative writer with his own 'vision' of life and his own utterance; Leavis is 'only' a superb literary critic. But creative writing and critical writing are not simple 'opposites', it is not a case of one being 'positive' and the other 'negative'; though in saying that either mode at its fullest may partake of something of the other's activity, we are by no means trying to equate two very different activities; and the creative artist's criticism is

likely to be in some ways of a different kind from the
critic's. The subject is too abstruse to be developed at length
here. But it can at least be pointed out that Lawrence the
creative artist was also a most sensitive and scrupulous
literary critic, and that Leavis the literary critic is ultimately
concerned with the vitality, the richness, the quality, of life
and living. It is significant that Leavis, so often attacked for
so-called pedantic analysis, has been one of the strongest
and most discriminating (and strong because discriminating)
upholders of Lawrence's intense and abundantly-alive
genius.

Lawrence flays the kind of analysis that characteristically
deals with counting syllables and describing rhyme-schemes
and naming metres and stanza-forms. And it still seems
necessary to insist, after all the fine critical work of the past
twenty or thirty years, that real literary analysis has no
affinities with grammatical sentence-analysis. Its accuracy is
not that of classification. It is that of a delicate discernment
and assessment of the experience, of the 'felt life' (Henry
James's phrase) in and behind the words that are being
examined. Those who misunderstand or fear literary analysis
tend to attack it for being 'niggling', or for 'murdering to
dissect', whereas the truth is that it helps to demonstrate the
wholeness of meaning, the total effect and significance of the
writing. And in doing this it adds immeasurably to the
pleasure as to the profit of reading.

If we take a characteristic passage from a work and find
it to be muddled in thought, then it is no use abstracting and
trusting to the ideas in that work; if a characteristic passage
is emotionally false or feeble, then we know it will be no use
going to the whole work to enhance our emotional experience. These are very elementary considerations; but some
people seem to think, in fact they will affirm, that a book can
be valuable *as literature* even if its actual *writing* is weak or
bad. They will give contents and writing separate treatment.
Comments like the following – this one is taken from a
newspaper – are frequent in reviews: 'This is a book that is
full of the wisdom of the English countryside, of humanity
and humour, and of writing that could scarcely be bet-

tered.' It is plain that the critic who wrote this, isolating certain qualities that he claims for his author, separating them off from the actual writing, has an inadequate conception of literature; his praise is in fact worthless, for if the writing were poor the wisdom and so on wouldn't be there. ('Full of the wisdom of the English countryside' is ambiguous: it could refer to the 'traditional' wisdom of country folk. But from the way the whole sentence is worded it seems certain that he is claiming for his author the great and rare quality of wisdom along with the humanity and humour.)

Writers are all too often judged by their explicit content. For instance: a 'left-wing' critic champions Shelley for his revolutionary doctrines; a 'right-wing' critic champions Tennyson for his nationalism; another critic champions Milton for his explicit moral or religious beliefs. Such critics are supporting their poets because they find in them support for their own beliefs or opinions (though they might not be ready to admit this); they are not sufficiently concerned with the 'sensibility' of the poets, their way of experiencing and expressing life, as revealed in the way they use words; they miss the *reality* of their authors. Sincere analysis would reveal disconcerting flaws in their idols' supposed strengths; it would cause a painful revision of opinions. Incidentally, it might also reveal excellences previously unrecognized. Mr Leavis's paragraph about 'relevance of response' seems to me to state admirably the central point in literary criticism: it is in the words of the writer, in his choice and ordering and organization of language, that his worth shows itself; as a literary artist expressing experiences worth our deepest attention, he matters there or not at all. When Bernard Shaw, writing about *Othello* in 1897, said 'To the brain it is ridiculous, to the ear it is sublime' (and he was echoed in 1948 by Mr Godfrey Tearle, playing the name-part), he was approaching literature in a manner characteristic of many rationalists: that is to say, he split the play into two elements, one of 'content' and one of 'poetry', in particular, poetry as it appeals by its sound only. Such a reading betrays failure to grasp what Shakespeare intended and what he achieved in the play. Most of Shaw's criticism of Shakespeare depends upon his separation of content from what he usually calls rhetoric, and his judging of each in separation. One of the main endeavours of this book will be to show that good writing is never a matter of embellishing unimportant or paltry content with a 'fine style'.

A critic has to be careful not to use the 'jargon' of criticism thoughtlessly. It is easy to collect a few words like 'sensibility', 'awareness', 'consciousness', and to make a show of adequacy with them. And yet we must have some such terms for practical use, to make discussion possible. The good critic will use them carefully and honestly. It will not be out of place to refer here to one or two of the current critical terms, especially as their meaning differs in some cases considerably from that which the same word bears in common use. 'Subtle', for instance, has not in criticism the commonly understood meaning of 'consciously calculating', but implies something sensitively delicate, delicate in the sense of the opposite of crude; the word 'precise', which in everyday use tends to be connected, often derogatorily, with a formal exactitude, is in criticism used as an 'approving' term for shades of emotion as well as for clarity of thought; 'profound' is the antithesis of 'shallow' as applied to emotion or intellect or to both working together; 'sophisticated' is not 'knowingly up-to-date' but implies in criticism the antithesis of 'naïve'. The critic then, especially when he is being explicitly educative, has to have recourse to some set of terms; 'jargon' can't be avoided. But he will see to it, when he uses one of the 'accepted' words, that he has before him the occasion for its use in the writing of the author whom he is helping to reveal; the 'critical' word matters *only* because it helps to reveal the author. It may be useful, valuable, to say that a 'sophisticated' mind is at work in Marvell's poetry; and in some circumstances of discussion the remark may not need enlarging upon. But the *essential* task of the critic is to discover, to *uncover* for us, those particular qualities and that particular working of the mind which justify the use of the adjective. He must *show* the 'sophisticated' mind in all its interesting activity.

A knowledge of the terms used in critical practice has in

itself nothing to do with keenly and freshly responding to a piece of writing. But, conversely, neither does a rigorous training in literary criticism inhibit a fresh and spontaneous response. On the contrary, the better trained we are the more truly and swiftly and pleasurably shall we appreciate and spontaneously evaluate what our author is offering us. And the more we are aware of the particular thing the author is offering, the better it is for our own intellectual and emotional growth. For the moment the claims of these statements must remain simply as claims; it is hoped that adequate justification for them will be felt later in the book.

The method of this book was decided on for the purpose of making demonstration as clear as possible. A good piece of writing, in fact any piece of writing, can be said to be a fusion of elements, and to abstract one element, rhythm for example, or imagery, and to discuss it in comparative isolation, can only be justified on the grounds indicated in our previous sentence. However, a more comprehensive analysis of the pieces quoted in the 'sections' can be made if desired, as well as of the twenty or so passages given later.

Many of the examined passages are excerpts; but I have tried to ensure in every case that the selection should be characteristic, in one way or another, of the author, and I have aimed at avoiding passages the criticism of which would depend to a considerable extent on its context. Especially in the criticism of a passage from a play or a novel we must feel sure about the author's intention: for it may be very different from that which a superficial reading might suggest. To give a clear example: it is irrelevant to charge Shakespeare with bombast when we are reading or listening to some of Othello's speeches; for the bombast is consciously *used*, and Shakespeare shows himself to be, by the whole meaning of the play taking in action and dialogue, the finest critic of his 'hero's' inflations.

Although the selected passages are characteristic of some salient features of their author, no inclusive judgement of any author is intended unless it is actually stated. This book by its intention comes almost entirely into the second category of the critic's work as given at the beginning of this note, and fundamental judgements and appraisals of an author's whole *œuvre* are outside its scope: we can feel by contact with a single paragraph how fine Conrad can be, but we cannot say we 'know' Conrad until we have grasped the novels as wholes.

The aims of our several Sections can be briefly set out: the first, on Rhythm, points out the difference between a rhythm that is expressive, that has a positive and meaningful and subtle function, and a rhythm that has been adopted mainly or solely for its surface 'musical' value; and the second section's aim is similar in that it examines some ways in which Rhyme is really *used* and some rhyme which is weak or bad. Section three is chiefly concerned with the aptness, the vividness, the suggestiveness of Imagery; again, an expressive use as against an ornamental device. The Poetic Thought section endeavours to distinguish between the statement of 'thoughts' or ideas and the nature of the thought that we call 'poetic'; the implications of 'poetic' are shown to involve feeling and the senses. The gist of the next section is the distinction between emotion and emotionalism, and there is discussion of 'implicit' feeling in language. The Diction section deals with the general 'superiority' of the concrete to the abstract word, and with 'poetic diction' and with the use in poetry of the language spoken in the poet's own day. The final section gives an opportunity of comparing and appraising a number of passages in verse and prose.

Teachers have their own ways of using text-books. With the present one, I myself cannot see a better course than to go through it page by page with the pupils. If time doesn't allow of this, and pupils have to read some or much of it by themselves, there can still follow plentiful discussion in the classroom. That is the essential thing, wherever it is possible: discussion. Close and detailed discussion whether between two or twenty people cannot be anything but profitable. In the second of the epigraphs to this book, Henry James was addressing young novelists; but his words are perfectly applicable to reading. James is one of those who have insisted that our best way of being 'generous' to a writer is to come by 'delicate' reading to a full appreciation of what he has written.

I believe that most of what may be found valuable in this book derives from the work of F. R. Leavis in modern literary criticism. Other 'influences' there are too, of course: Mr T. S. Eliot, Mr Middleton Murry, Mr I. A. Richards, Mr William Empson, and others. By giving our attention to the criticism of the best critics (ultimately to their best criticism), we can help ourselves to become good, full readers. And the ability to read is a great thing to have; especially in these times when such a quantity of print is expended on such a variety of purposes.

Chapter 1

RHYTHM

A COMMON misconception about rhythm in writing, a misconception which misleads some writers and which some writers exploit, is that which neatly and too exclusively relates it to other kinds of rhythm, such as the beating of the heart, the motion of the arms and legs in walking, the alternation of day and night, of the seasons, the moon's passage round the earth, the earth's round the sun. This more or less regular recurrence of functions and activities of man and nature and the universe is often held to be the foundation of rhythm in art. Such an account errs because it makes mere repetition the active principle, as if the rhythm of art were essentially the same as the rhythm formed by the exact repetition of the units which make up a design on wallpaper. The flaw in the analogy is that by it rhythm in writing becomes only a matter of methodical timing and mechanical emphasis; the account omits *real* emphasis, the meaningful emphasis of words given by the quality and pressure of the emotion and thought behind the words. Good rhythm, which means really the most effectual *movement*, comes from an interplay of this real emphasis with the *rate* of movement, the tempo, of the word-sequence.

It is obvious that if our normal speech were to develop a quite regular pattern of utterance the result would be intolerably uniform; language would have become a dead thing. As a matter of fact such a pattern, in speaking, is almost unimaginable; it can hardly be imposed even by the most rigid conscious effort. The infinitely rich complexity of human emotion and intellectual activity gives an infinite range of inflexion and tone to the commonest everyday speech; the attitude, the feeling, that determines the tone of the speech, often determines also the way in which the words are stressed as well as their rate of movement: tone, stress and tempo are fused. Think of the ways in which even a commonplace like 'Good morning' can be said. The rhythm of our everyday language is always and continuously being given subtle variations by our shifts of feeling and mood, by our interest and the kind of interest in what we are saying, or by our lack of interest; and under the stress of powerful and complex feelings how much more suggestive and variable does the rhythm become.

Depth (not necessarily vehemence) of feeling and conviction impels the best writers to write in a more marked rhythm than that of ordinary speech. But it is dangerously easy to manufacture an obvious kind of rhythm, to make up a kind of sing-song that is but a poor substitute for real rhythm; and this kind of writing, especially in poetry, has had far more attention paid to it than it deserves. People in general like easily understood and perhaps easily memorable writing: jingles in poetry, practically useful like 'Thirty days hath September', and 'useless' like 'Hickory Dickory Dock', are popular. We like these jingles, and they do their work well; but we don't expect more serious writing to be so set and symmetrical. 'More attention than it deserves': this was said because the tendency to treat poetry as predominantly a musical sing-song has to a considerable extent helped to obstruct the recognition and enjoyment and right understanding of a great deal of good, and great, writing.

We can start our examination of several short pieces with a few lines from one of Swinburne's best-known poems – a chorus from his drama *Atalanta*. The poet is enthusiastically celebrating the passing of 'winter's rains and ruins' and the new warmth of 'the southwest-wind and the west-wind':

> *... And in green underwood and cover*
> *Blossom by blossom the spring begins.*
>
> *The full streams feed on flower of rushes,*
> * Ripe grasses trammel a travelling foot,*
> *The faint fresh flame of the young year flushes*
> * From leaf to flower and flower to fruit;*
> *And fruit and leaf are as gold and fire,*
> *And the oat is heard above the lyre,*
> *And the hoofèd heel of a satyr crushes*
> * The chestnut-husk at the chestnut-root.*

And Pan by noon and Bacchus by night,
Fleeter of foot than the fleet-foot kid,
Follows with dancing and fills with delight
The Maenad and the Bassarid ...

The question we are concerned with at the moment is: how, and for what ends, is the poet using rhythm? From these lines it appears quite clearly that the sound of the words is his first consideration; and if we could have heard Swinburne himself reading his verse it would have been all the more obvious that, whatever his subject matter, it was the music of words that absorbed nearly all his attention. Read these lines aloud and you will find the rhythmical pattern to be very insistent in its regularity; line is balanced with line, and the line itself is frequently divided into two evenly weighted phrases. Alliteration, assonance, and repetition are all worked in for the final musical effect. Swinburne, indulging in what may be called poetical incantation, induces in many readers the romantic pleasure of surrendering to a kind of spell; and his skill in this direction is extraordinary. And there is often a buoyancy and ardour in his metrical flow through which the poet's ardent spirit is felt. But we have doubts about the ultimate value of this kind of writing as soon as we throw off the incantatory influence and attend more closely to *what* the poet is saying. And what do we find in our present example? Surely that the sense of the passage is vague and uncertain, that it seems in places to be left to look after itself: it is all the time subordinate to the lilt of the verse. Does spring begin with *blossoms* in underwood and cover that the poet himself says is already green? Would Swinburne have written that if he had had, or had kept in mind a clear vision of the first tentative putting forth of spring's beginnings and if he had had a firm intention of describing it? We are not 'splitting hairs' in asking such questions; for after all, the poet is supposed to be telling us about spring. Again: the whole of the stanza beginning with 'The full streams feed' seems to have spring, summer, and autumn all in one; consider some of the details and you will find it impossible to say what time of the year Swinburne is describing. He is lax in his attention to the sense of his words, and exact in his management of the metre. Notice how each of the last four lines quoted is almost exactly divided into two metrically and musically equal parts, the alliteration adding to the effect of even balance. The exaggeration of the simile about the 'fleet-foot kid' doesn't much matter in a reference to gods like Pan and Bacchus; but another interesting point arises here: whether Swinburne is describing fast or slow movements his rhythm maintains almost exactly a uniform speed throughout. As he consciously aimed at this effect we cannot say he failed; on the contrary. But we can question the value of the aim; and we can also say that this use of rhythm, calling attention to itself all the time, runs the risk of quickly becoming monotonous. A finer poet would certainly care more about the real value of movement in his verse than to allow a line about the foot being impeded by thick grass to move along so trippingly as Swinburne's does. Not that we expect onomatopoeia to be present in all poetry; but unless we are careless readers I do not think we shall be satisfied for long with such a symmetrical pattern, however musical, as Swinburne imposes on his subject matter, giving the same rhythmical value to all his statements. The great writer uses rhythm to indicate the relative value and significance of his perceptions and feelings and thoughts; he has intensities, pauses, quiet places; his rhythm helps to convey the full weight of his meaning and experience. Swinburne's rhythm, attractive and splendid as it often is in itself, tends to blur his content and to tempt the reader to pay little attention to its frequent vaguenesses, confusions, and inaccuracies.

Another and more obviously deplorable use or misuse of rhythm occurs when a writer claiming to express sincere feeling uses a form manufactured for the occasion, a form which will be found to betray a falsity or emptiness of feeling. (Most popular songs could be glanced at in this connexion.) When Dryden writes:

> *Hope is banished,*
> *Joys are vanished,*
> *Damon, my beloved, is gone!*

we do not feel that the words carry any great sense of loss. Loss of hope and of joy, the feeling of bereavement, do not express themselves in such abrupt and perfunctory measures. An example of the same tendency, but more interesting and less simple, comes from Poe's famous 'The Raven':

> *Ah! distinctly I remember, it was in the bleak December,*
> *And each separate dying ember wrought its ghost upon the floor.*
> *Eagerly I wished the morrow; vainly I had sought to borrow*
> *From my books surcease of sorrow — sorrow for the lost Lenore —*
> *For the rare and radiant maiden whom the angels name Lenore —*
> *Nameless here for evermore.*

The feeling of hopelessness in the face of loss is perhaps conveyed here more impressively than in the fragment from Dryden; but as it is rhythm that we are examining, we shall not point to such things as the bleak background and the reference to the vain consolation of books as factors making for Poe's superiority. We have to ask, How far does the rhythm help to express the gloom and sorrow connected in the poet's memory with 'the lost Lenore'? And when we do this we feel that some of the points made about Swinburne may be made about Poe also, the main one being that he has an excessive interest in the sound of the sequence of words, sound for its own sake, and excessive because it is in fact almost monopolistic. In this instance we do feel a certain hollow gloom about the whole sound of the stanza which is some indication of the poet's state of mind; and the monotony of the movement perhaps reflects the monotony of his existence. But though there may be behind the poem an experience of poignant personal suffering we find that when this comes to be uttered in verse it changes into something very different: and this is, a gloomy pleasure in making a carefully musical lament. For surely the rhythm does here try to cast a spell on the reader, it beats away incessantly and regularly. The rather mechanical construction of the stanza — notice that there are nine phrases or clauses all of the same rhythmical value — is evidence of a self-conscious effort rather than of deep impulsion from within. Poe makes the rhythm take charge in its own right, and becomes careless of meaning: hence the very doubtful sense of the second line; hence also the third line, employing the same dreary movement to suggest eagerness as to suggest the futility of reading: the statement 'eagerly I wished the morrow' doesn't ring true at all, it just chimes in with the other mournful clauses and phrases. The last line but one, with its idealistic but commonplace sentiment, also seems to quarrel with itself: it uses words intended to be highly impressive – 'rare' and 'radiant' – to describe Lenore; but so mechanically has Poe established his rhythm that they slip by without any more emphasis than any of the others; the slick movement works directly against the intention of the poet to make a paragon of Lenore. And this is the greatest defect of a too-regular rhythm: that it prevents the expression of the subtle shifts and shades of feeling and attitude which belong to the true and vivid description of almost every experience. Poe's set stanza is too much on one note, it lacks a living movement and so lacks life.

Now here is the first stanza of Donne's 'Nocturnall upon St Lucies Day, being the shortest day':

> *'Tis the yeares midnight, and it is the dayes,*
> *Lucies, who scarce seaven houres herself unmaskes,*
> *The Sunne is spent, and now his flasks*
> *Send forth light squibs, no constant rayes;*
>   *The worlds whole sap is sunke:*
> *The generalle balme th' hydroptique earth hath drunke,*
> *Whither, as to the beds-feet, life is shrunke,*
> *Dead and enterr'd; yet all these seeme to laugh,*
> *Compar'd with mee who am their epitaph.*

The feeling that inspires the poem is one of loss and profound dejection at the death of his lover; and it is apparent from the start that we are dealing with something very different from the ordinary run of mournful love-poems. The poet is writing at midnight on the shortest day of the year; the sun's strength at this season appears only in intermittent feeble gleams; all the sap and moisture of plants and trees has sunk back into the huge water-swollen earth; the agents of life (for instance, flowers) have shrivelled and died; yet the gloom of none of these things can compare with that of the poet, whose heavy task it is to consider and record their fate. Such is, briefly, the prose-content of the stanza, a content which we shall find to be superbly fused with and given emotional force by the rhythmical expression. Now what is it that we feel immediately in the movement of this poetry as differing from that of Poe, who was also concerned with a personal loss? The various answers that could be given to this question might be unified into this one, a negative one for the moment: it is not incantatory. If you tried to reduce the movement of this verse to anything like incantation you would produce ridiculous effects. But read it as the poet has written it, giving attention to the stresses and pauses, and you will feel something quite distinct from the facile movement of the extracts previously examined: you will feel the power of rhythm to convey and reinforce the emotion and thought-content of the words. And all is done without the least sense of artificial forcing. The first line is very quiet, the lack of emphasis suggesting the low spirit of the poet, though there is something quietly solemn even in that colourless second part of the line. Then the voice comes down on 'Lucies' with more weight, stressing it: in addition to giving the name of this day which is so full of significance for the poet, Donne wishes to convey the hint of irony that he feels in the word, which has connexions in his mind with 'lucid' and 'lucent': the atmosphere and temper of the time is anything but that to Donne. The slow and laborious movement of 'who scarce seaven houres', coming after the comma and pause, reproduces a sense of difficulty and obstruction in the sun's efforts to appear; there is for the poet no bright energy in nature's operations at this season. The very source of life is 'spent' (later in the poem, we feel an added intensity in this thought when the poet states that his own sun, the lost one, can never renew itself). The fourth line is remarkable in that every word receives emphasis, every syllable except one: but note the thin sounds in the rather contemptuous phrase 'light squibs' as against the sure, broad vowels of 'no constant rayes': the heavy 'no', with 'rayes', especially emphasizes the lifeless and negative quality of despair, despair that is in this in-

stance deep and understood, not wild and incoherent. The
fifth line is extremely slow and heavy with the poet's spirit
and with the sodden weight of the earth. There is some
quickening in lines six and seven as the poet gives an image
of the thirsty earth, absorbing everything inevitably; but
then fall the three heavy words 'shrunke', 'dead', and 'en-
terr'd', words of such intense meaning in the poet's imagination, for they refer to a loved person's body as well as to the
general 'life' of natural things at this season. After this
solemnity there is a lighter movement rising to the unexpected word 'laugh', and passing into an easy but
deliberate conversationalism in 'Compar'd with mee'. Then
the last four words resume the steady inevitability. The
emphasis on the tiny word 'am' is not only to indicate the
certainty of the fact that he is the epitaph, the recorder of
these melancholy things; it also gives greater point to the
paradox of his being the worst-off of all although he is still
alive – I AM, they are NOT, and yet I am in a worse state
than they.

A full analysis of the stanza would of course reveal further
profundity and wealth of meaning; I have restricted myself
to its rhythm as far as was possible (and have not examined,
for instance, the significance of words like 'flasks', 'whole',
'hydroptique', and of the ambiguity of 'light', and of that
sudden, surprising simile 'as to the beds-feet'). And the
essential point that emerges is this: that Donne does not use
rhythm as a musical attraction that is likely to confuse or
lessen the significance of what he is saying. He is not more
concerned with the 'how' than with the 'what': all is one
in Donne. The movement follows the direction of the emotion and the thought; it is not imposed rigidly and as it
were ready-made on the material; it seems to rise inevitably
out of the poet's feeling and attitude. It is organic, not
separable; living and varied, not mechanical. It is the reverse of sing-song in that it is based on the flexibility of the
living spoken language. And ultimately this functional
rhythm has a far deeper and finer and more complex
'music' than any incantation can provide.

A passage from drama may serve for further comparison

and contrast. Volumnia, type of the Roman matron, is persuading her son Coriolanus to return to the plebeians and humbly apologize for his previous angry pride and scorn before them (she hates them as much as he does):

> *I prithee now, my son,*
> *Go to them, with this bonnet in thy hand;*
> *And thus far having stretcht it — here be with them —*
> *Thy knee bussing the stones — for in such business*
> *Action is eloquence, and the eyes of the ignorant*
> *More learned than the ears — waving thy head,*
> *Which often, thus, correcting thy stout heart,*
> *Now humble as the ripest mulberry*
> *That will not hold the handling — or say to them*
> *Thou art their soldier, and, being bred in broils,*
> *Hast not the soft way which, thou dost confess,*
> *Were fit for thee to use, as they to claim,*
> *In asking their good loves; but thou wilt frame*
> *Thyself, forsooth, hereafter theirs, so far*
> *As thou hast power and person.*

The essential characteristic of the rhythm here is its dramatic variety and persuasiveness: it helps to present and it reflects masterfully the intention of the speaker, and it is used also in such a way as to emphasize certain points about the whole theme of the play and about the character of Coriolanus. Volumnia enjoys this speech; acting, as she goes along, the part she is counselling her son to play, she builds up with point after point, sometimes not waiting to complete a sentence. Her pauses and little interjections, her changes of approach and of method of appeal, are all present in the rhythm of the speech (which is really one long sentence). A line by line analysis is unnecessary, but a few details may be noted. The stressed 'my son' in the first line is both a maternal appeal and a reminder of an important element in the play's thought: that is, that Coriolanus in his pride and hard insensitiveness is the true son of the war-like and unfeminine Roman matron. 'Go', in its place of importance at the beginning of a line, is as much command as pleading. The little aside 'here be with them', is cajoling, and with what follows forms a very telling expression of

Volumnia's manner: the rhythm is plausible and calculating like her advice. The powerful phrase 'Action is eloquence' comes out boldly, and 'eyes' and 'ears' have their appropriate weight in this definitive axiom-like statement. The solid sound of 'stout heart', further stressed by the comma that follows it, contrasts with the soft and smooth movement of the ripe mulberry simile, which suggests beautifully the softness of the fruit and the (precarious) humility of the conduct she is advising, as well as her own assumed blandness. Then she breaks off sharply with another idea: 'soldier' has emphasis, and the hard, mouth-filling 'bred in broils', so truly descriptive of Coriolanus's upbringing, is set off against the next line and a half, which (from 'hast' to 'use') has, with its sibilant sounds, an insinuating quality about it. 'Good loves' is scornfully ironical. In the penultimate line, 'thyself' and 'theirs' are strongly linked rhythmically as well as alliteratively. The stressed words of the last line, 'power' and 'person', again point to the theme of Coriolanus's power and personality. As always in good poetry, the sounds of words, the suggestiveness of the sound of single words and of word-sequences, are linked organically with the rhythm. The rhythm here has its roots in the spoken language; it is the presence of the modulations of the speaking voice that gives the passage its lithe, complex movement. It is flexible and dramatic rhythm, and it does its work unobtrusively and with full spontaneous ease. Its seeming simplicity is deceptive; one might write a thousand lines in Poe's manner more easily than five in this.

The specimens of writing that have so far been examined in this section illustrate two radically different ways of using rhythm. I have tried to show in what ways the more varied and complex rhythm indicates a richer and more varied play of mind and feeling behind the words: it expresses more, and it expresses more adequately. For the past two centuries or so the view of poetry as *par excellence* incantation has become very common, and it is perhaps this, mainly, that has brought poetry to appear a comparatively trifling thing in the 'general mind'. Of course, good use can be made of incantatory measures; and in lighter kinds of verse they are often extremely effective. Many of our early street-ballads, for example, have a lively and rollicking incantatory rhythm. Hood's lilting punning-poems can give much pleasure; here is a part of 'Ben Bluff':

> Ben Bluff was a whaler, and many a day
> Had chased the huge fish about Baffin's old Bay;
> But time brought a change his division to spoil,
> And that was when Gas took the shine out of Oil.
>
> He turn'd up his nose at the fumes of the coke,
> And swore the whole scheme was a bottle of smoke;
> As to London he briefly delivered his mind,
> 'Sparm-city,' said he – but the City declined.
>
> So Ben cut his line in a sort of a huff,
> As soon as his Whales had brought profits enough,
> And hard by the Docks settled down for his life,
> But, true to his text, went to Wales for a wife.
>
> A big one she was, without figure or waist,
> More bulky than lovely, but that was his taste;
> In fat she was lapp'd from her sole to her crown,
> And, turn'd into oil would have lighted a town.
>
> But Ben like a Whaler was charm'd with the match,
> And thought, very truly, his spouse a great catch;
> A flesh-and-blood emblem of Plenty and Peace,
> And would not have changed her for Helen of Greece.
>
> For Greenland was green in his memory still;
> He'd quitted his trade, but retain'd the good-will;
> And often when soften'd by bumbo and flip,
> Would cry – till he blubber'd – about his old ship.

The poet's nimble word-play, which is by no means always spotted at a first reading, is well contained in the easy, unserious lilt of the movement. Then again: the simple imitative movement of poems like 'How they Brought the Good News' and 'The Assyrian Came down like a Wolf on the Fold' is admirably appropriate for their purpose of simple-exciting narrative. But for the recording of the most valuable and richest experiences such measures are inadequate. Sometimes a great poet does use a more or less regular rhythmical pattern (though probably never such a rigid one as Swinburne's or Poe's or Hood's) for subtle expression – Marvell, for instance, and Blake, and Yeats – but it is never felt in these (in their best work, that is) that the sound is calling out for the chief attention; the qualities that go to make up the wisdom of their 'singing' include the knowledge or instinct to make the sound an integral part of their whole meaning and intention. W. B. Yeats, in an essay, refers to 'the defects of my early poetry; I insisted upon obvious all-pervading rhythm'. Further opportunity will be found for considering the rhythm of various pieces by these last-named poets and others, in later sections of the book.

Rhythm, as an active factor, is of course not so apparent in prose as in verse. The great bulk of all prose written is of the informative or expository or argumentative kinds, and the rhythm of such writing tends to be of a rather neutral quality; though even a piece of abstract scientific writing suffers if its rhythm is altogether inert. A formal and excessively marked verse-rhythm is hardly more deplorable than continuous rhythmical lifelessness in prose. The rhythmical qualities of great and good prose are comparable with those of fine poetry. A full examination of such is outside the scope of this book; but the section may be closed with two examples of prose where rhythm is powerfully used to reinforce the content, to add an emotional richness to the prose-meaning, to carry home to the reader the writer's attitude and feelings and thoughts; in each instance the rhythm is an inseparable part of the total meaning and effect. First, a few verses from the Book of Job:

> *Canst thou draw out leviathan with an hook? or his tongue with a cord which thou lettest down?*
> *Canst thou put an hook into his nose? or bore his jaw through with a thorn?*
> *Will he make many supplications unto thee? will he speak soft words unto thee?*
> *Will he make a covenant with thee? wilt thou take him for a servant for ever?*
> *Wilt thou play with him as with a bird? or wilt thou bind him for thy maidens?*

Shall the companions make a banquet of him? shall they part him
  among the merchants?
Canst thou fill his skin with barbed irons? or his head with fish
  spears?

Read this aloud and the impact of the writer's theme will be
closely and immediately felt through the stress that falls,
and falls with the natural emphasis of 'passionate' speech, on
all the key words, words which in connexion with the
image of the great whale are used with powerful scorn: the
rhythm conveys, working with the prose-meaning, the
writer's attitude; he knows with certainty that there is no
answer to any of his questions except 'no'. But scorn for
man's pretensions is not the only feeling here: there is a
corresponding sense of exultation in the creativeness of God
or Nature, and a sense of power is felt through the rhythm.
Note the impressiveness of the way in which the first question is put, with the slow, dragging words to suggest the
drawing out of the whale followed by the mocking little
'hook'; and the similar effect, the physical task being so hard
and slow as to be impossible, in 'bore his jaw through with a
thorn'; and how 'soft words', 'play', 'banquet', and several
more words and phrases are emphasized with irony as a
challenge to man's capacities. And these individual effects
are contained in a rhythm which, although it has a certain
'pattern', has also a powerful and weighty flow.

Our second example is no less magnificent. D. H.
Lawrence is describing the life amid which the Brangwen
family have lived for generations:

So the Brangwens came and went without fear of necessity, working hard because of the life that was in them, not for want of the
money. Neither were they thriftless. They were aware of the last
halfpenny, and instinct made them not waste the peeling of their
apple, for it would help to feed the cattle. But heaven and earth
was teeming around them, and how should this cease? They felt
the rush of the sap in spring, they knew the wave which cannot
halt, but every year throws forward the seed to begetting, and,
falling back, leaves the young-born on the earth. They knew the
intercourse between heaven and earth, sunshine drawn into the
breast and bowels, the rain sucked up in the daytime, nakedness

that comes under the wind in autumn, showing the birds' nests no longer worth hiding. Their life and interrelations were such; feeling the pulse and body of the soil, that opened to their furrow for the grain, and became smooth and supple after their ploughing, and clung to their feet with a weight that pulled like desire, lying hard and unresponsive when the crops were to be shorn away. The young corn waved and was silken, and the lustre slid along the limbs of the men who saw it. They took the udder of the cows, the cows yielded milk and pulse against the hands of the men, the pulse of the blood of the teats of the cows beat into the pulse of the hands of the men. They mounted their horses, and held life between the grip of their knees, they harnessed their horses at the wagon, and, with hand on the bridle-rings, drew the heaving of the horses after their will.

The early lines about the work and thrift of the Brangwens are even and quiet in movement, though 'came and went' gives a sense of the continuity of the family as if it were part of nature's continuity, as in a way it is; and there is a significant balance between two phrases: 'because of the life that was in them', and 'not for want of the money', where the words 'life', 'not', and 'money', stand out. But when Lawrence begins, at 'But heaven and earth ...', to describe the natural forces of which 'they', the Brangwens, are a part, the writing becomes informed with a superb rhythm which seems to have a pulse of its own and to move with the triumphant inevitability of the processes that it presents. As an illuminating contrast, the Donne stanza may be recalled with its masterly, slow and deliberate movement; here, clause follows clause with strong, living movement, reflecting and presenting Lawrence's positive attitude towards life, whereas Donne's was in a sense negative. In even an average reading of the passage, the voice will stress all the significant words giving images of nature's abundant power and her continuity in change and of man's place and work among them. A few details from many may be noted: the sentence beginning 'The young corn waved ...' flows along with the ease and smoothness that it describes; while the rhythm of the following sentence is itself like a powerful pulse. 'Drew the heaving of the horses after their will' works by its movement and sound in a way similar to that of

'Canst thou draw out leviathan', suggesting muscular exertion and physical strength. In fact, there is throughout a feeling of 'body' in the rhythm, of body combined with invigorating movement, and it is this combination, going of course with the controlled profusion of the sensuous images that figure nature's fundamental processes, that gives this writing its extraordinary strength. It would be instructive to glance back at the first extract quoted in this section. By the side of Lawrence's exhilarating reality and beauty, Swinburne's 'faint fresh flame of the young year' appears a rather pale poetical fabrication.

Chapter 2

RHYME

To say that rhyme is not an essential element in poetry is not to belittle its importance; nearly all the English poets who have written memorable rhymeless verse have also on other occasions used rhyme memorably. Used: that is the important word. For rhyme had far better be absent from a poem if it is not doing something effectively; if it is not fulfilling any worth-while function it is only an empty convention or an affectation. The common fallacy that poetry is rhyming and that rhyming is poetry, is as preventive of the understanding of the nature of poetry as the belief that rhythm in poetry is jog-trot or mechanical movement. With the help of a rhyming dictionary almost any literate person can concoct a 'poem'; and it doesn't need genius for a writer to become very fluent in the practice of rhyming. But to *use* rhyme for emphasis and point, for enhancing the intensity and subtlety of meaning, for evoking the feeling in the reader that the poet's expression is the inevitably right one (and all this without any suggestion of words having been juggled into a self-consciously arranged pattern), is beyond the reach of mere versifiers. Such uses of rhyme are often most unobtrusive in the way they function. But it will be best to begin with a kind of writing in which rhyming has clearly a prominent role, namely the heroic couplet.

> *Great wits are sure to madness near allied,*
> *And thin partitions do their bounds divide.*

Dryden's aim in this celebrated couplet was to make a neat formulation of an interesting psychological 'truth'. He knew well the effectiveness of the rhyming couplet for such a purpose, and he produced in this one a deservedly admired and much-quoted specimen. But the couplet is not so sparkling as it appears to be, if we consider it as expressive

utterance: the second line adds nothing in thought to the
first, and this is some defect in a couplet which obviously
aims at expressing a thought succinctly; also, 'divide',
which naturally receives and seems intended to receive considerable stress as the rhyming and final word, emphasizes
division, whereas the poet is actually concerned with the idea
of association: the second line says virtually the same thing
as the first, but the rhyming words 'allied' and 'divide' convey opposite impressions. By stressing 'thin', however, and
treating 'divide' as lightly as possible, the intended meaning is obtained. The blemish does little to invalidate the
couplet's interest as the neat vehicle of an idea; it nevertheless provides a good example of a rhyme which contributes
nothing positive to the whole expression.

In Pope's couplet:

> *Know, Nature's children all divide her care;*
> *The fur that warms a monarch, warm'd a bear.*

the rhyme is used to more advantage. The couplet gives first
the general thought, then a concrete exemplification of the
thought. In the second line, it is especially the rhymed word,
belonging to the picturesque particular example, that gives
an incisiveness to the general idea. 'Bear' is stressed both as
forceful contrast to 'monarch' (a contrast all the more
relevant in Pope's day when the bear-pit showed the animal
in dreadful degradation; the reference to a bear would immediately evoke an image or associations in most readers of
that time) and as being identical with the monarch in its
dependence on Nature's 'care'.

Here is a longer passage from Pope; he is satirizing, in
one of his Epistles, the bad taste of all classes attending the
theatre of his time:

> *There still remains, to mortify a Wit,*
> *The many-headed Monster of the Pit:*
> *A senseless, worthless, and unhonour'd crowd;*
> *Who, to disturb their betters mighty proud,*
> *Clatt'ring their sticks before ten lines are spoke,*
> *Call for the Farce, the Bear, or the Black-joke.*
> *What dear delight to Britons Farce affords!*
> *Ever the taste of Mobs, but now of Lords;*

(Taste, that eternal wanderer, which flies
From heads to ears, and now from ears to eyes.)
The Play stands still; damn action and discourse,
Back fly the scenes, and enter foot and horse;
Pageants on Pageants, in long order drawn,
Peers, Heralds, Bishops, Ermine, Gold and Lawn;
The Champion too! and, to complete the jest,
Old Edward's Armour beams on Cibber's breast.
With laughter sure Democritus had died,
Had he beheld an Audience gape so wide.

The succinctness of the first couplet derives largely from the sharp rhymes 'Wit' and 'Pit': in Pope's day a Wit was a man of good education, of cultivated talents, and the word had associations strongly in opposition to those attaching to 'Pit'. 'Proud' in line four stands out ironically by virtue of the contrast it makes with the adjectives previously applied to the 'crowd' in line three. Then the 'Black-joke' is held up to ridicule (it was some kind of horseplay in which black-pudding figured) as the culminating absurdity of stage entertainment, where what is 'spoke' should be the essential source of the enjoyment. 'Lords', in the fourth couplet, is especially effective as being both contrast to and identity with 'Mobs' (the method is similar to that of the monarch-and-bear line). The bracketed couplet neatly refers to the deterioration in public taste: this taste, which 'flies' because it is a light and ephemeral thing lacking substantial quality, passed from head (plays) to ears (opera), and now it has sunk to eyes (mere spectacle); 'eyes' is appropriately stressed as the lowest point reached. The entrance of a 'horse', clumsy and mindless (from this point of view), on to the stage, is ludicrously set off against what ought to be there, namely proper stage-action and particularly 'discourse'; the anti-climax of 'enter foot and horse' is like a stage-direction for a battle-scene in full dress. Even the Church plays a part in this lavish display, the 'Lawn' of the Bishops' vestments being conspicuous in the long 'drawn' out spectacle. The 'breast' of Cibber, intended to be so noble and imposing in a king's armour (armour for a performance was borrowed from the Tower on one occasion) is perhaps the most ridiculous element in the whole great 'jest'. The laughing philosopher would surely have died with laughing, not only at such a show but even more at the sight of such an audience: 'wide' leaves us with a picture of mouths open with stupid astonishment. It will be seen that Pope has made use of no rhyming word simply by virtue of its property as sound-similarity. Each has a positive contribution to make towards the clear and definite statement, the precise satire, of the poet. A very valuable point in favour of the rhyming couplet, especially when used for satiric and aphoristic purposes, is that the end word of the first line remains echoing in the mind long enough for its fellow rhyming word, by confirmation or contrast or some other means of modification, to clinch the statement and bring home pertinently the full meaning and intention of the couplet. And the more 'accidental' the rhymes appear to be – given always their individual effectiveness, of course – the more inevitable-seeming will be the whole passage.

A rhyme that is in itself unduly obtrusive is evidence, usually, either that the author is incompetent or that he is in more or less frivolous mood. Browning has many bizarre rhymes, and they often tend to attract to themselves too much of our attention and so interfere with the total response we are intended by him to make to the whole poem. But in a semi-humorous poem like 'The Pied Piper' we are not put out by things like this:

> An hour they sat in Council;
> At length the Mayor broke silence;
> For a guilder I'd my ermine gown sell –
> I wish I were a mile hence.

And when Byron writes:

> But oh! ye lords of ladies intellectual!
> Inform us truly, have they not henpecked you all?

we can enjoy the contrast between the tones of the two lines, a contrast especially marked in the rhymes, even while we call the verse doggerel. Byron sometimes used uncouth rhymes through negligence and haste; but where they occur in his best work, as they frequently do, it is often with a fully conscious purpose: he can produce amusingly mocking effects by describing and reflecting on solemn affairs with a rhyming agility that appears flippant but that is really the servant of a serious intention.

What can happen to the work of anyone attempting to write serious rhyming poetry without a proper understanding of the use of rhyme, can be seen in these lines from Francis Mahony's much-anthologized 'Bells of Shandon':

> With deep affection,
> And recollection,
> I often think of
> Those Shandon bells,
> Whose sounds so wild would,
> In the days of childhood,
> Fling around my cradle
> Their magic spells.
> On this I ponder
> Where'er I wander,
> And thus grow fonder,
> Sweet Cork, of thee;
> With thy bells of Shandon,
> That sound so grand on
> The pleasant waters
> Of the River Lee.
>
> I've heard bells chiming
> Full many a clime in,
> Tolling sublime in
> Cathedral shrine,
> While at a glib rate
> Brass tongues would vibrate —
> But all their music
> Spoke nought like thine;
> For memory, dwelling
> On each proud swelling
> Of the belfry knelling
> Its bold notes free,
> Made the bells of Shandon
> Sound far more grand on
> The pleasant waters
> Of the River Lee.

These rhymes sound like an exercise in rhyming, and a rather crude one at that; and considered as an element of a poem which, the author tells us, is an utterance of feelings that he treasures, they become all the more defective: for they are too numerous and they are too insistent in sound, and in their insistence on calling attention to themselves merely as rhyming words, they distort the meaning and frequently become absurd or unnecessary. 'Recollection' is weakly redundant, going with line three. 'Wild would', an obviously manufactured rhyme, makes us question 'wild' as a suitable adjective, and gives undue weight to the unimportant 'would'. 'Magic spells' is the cliché ready-to-hand for 'bells'. 'Grand on', as part of the well-worn phrase 'sound grand', makes the feeblest of jingles with 'Shandon', as well as over-stressing 'on'. The second line of the second stanza is awkwardly manipulated for rhyme's sake. In fact, 'glib' is a poor word to make 'rate' tally with 'vibrate'. And so on. This examination of such palpably bad rhymes may seem a demonstration of the obvious; but it serves to show how false and muddled the expression of an experience or of a thought can become when merely a desire to write poetry is accepted as inspiration. No doubt the bells of Shandon did mean something to Mahony; but he failed to make poetry out of their significance for him. And perhaps the most apparent single symptom of his failure is his failure with rhymes.

A poet may be distinguished and yet not use rhymes with any great degree of sharp significance and wealth of suggestion. Many critics would agree that Tennyson's best work depends mainly on the musical beauty he created from a sensitive and dexterous management of words. At its best, this verbal music has an unquestionably individual accent. The following lines, expressing the desires of the mariners of the 'Lotos Eaters', and indicating the background against which they speak, are characteristic of this music:

> *How sweet it were, hearing the downward stream,*
> *With half-shut eyes ever to seem*
> *Falling asleep in a half-dream!*

To dream and dream, like yonder amber light,
Which will not leave the myrrh-bush on the height;
To hear each other's whisper'd speech;
Eating the Lotos day by day,
To watch the crisping ripples on the beach,
And tender curving lines of creamy spray;
To lend our hearts and spirits wholly
To the influence of mild-minded melancholy;
To muse and brood and live again in memory,
With those old faces of our infancy
Heap'd over with a mound of grass,
Two handfuls of white dust, shut in an urn of brass! ...

But propt on beds of amaranth and moly,
How sweet (while warm airs lull us, blowing lowly)
With half-dropt eyelids still,
Beneath a heaven dark and holy,
To watch the long bright river drawing slowly
His waters from the purple hill —
To hear the dewy echoes calling
From cave to cave thro' the thick-twined vine —
To watch the emerald-colour'd water falling
Thro' many a wov'n acanthus-wreath divine!
Only to hear and see the far-off sparkling brine,
Only to hear were sweet, stretch'd out beneath the pine.

The Lotus blooms below the barren peak:
The Lotus blows by every winding creek:
All day the wind breathes low with mellower tone:
Thro' every hollow cave and alley lone
Round and round the spicy downs the yellow Lotos-dust is blown.

The excellence of the rhymes here is that they are of a piece
with the total onomatopoeic excellence of the passage.
Tennyson's aim is not an ambitious one: it is to evoke,
mainly by the sound of words, the simple feeling of the
attractiveness of a sensuously idyllic life without effort and
action; but within its limits the poetry is admirable. Any
suggestion of vigorous movement would disturb the imagined peace, in the evocation of which the rhyming words
are used to great advantage. Nearly all are slow, soft,
languorous: a detailed analysis would show a remarkable

and effective predominance of long vowel sounds and of the consonants m, n, l, and s, and a high percentage of double rhymes with a 'falling' cadence. Only three rhyming words out of thirty-two seem to lack the pervasive quiet and dreaminess; of these 'brass' is intentionally a contrasting word in a momentarily contrasting idea, while 'peak' and 'creek' are easily absorbed into the surrounding mellowness. And of all these rhymes none is a mere insertion for convenience of rhyming; 'moly' (a lucky word for the poet, certainly), which at first might seem to be forced in, is found to be in harmony in a poem with lotos, myrrh, acanthus, amaranth. And all the rhymes are of equal importance in sound: this helps a great deal in diffusing the essential quality of ease and relaxed sensuousness evenly over the whole passage. Also, many of these rhyming words have a suggestiveness and associations (suitably vague in a mental, emotional, and physical-natural environment of this kind), which are appropriate to the general smoothness of the sounds of the words themselves: dream, melancholy, memory, still, holy, divine, pine (with its sweet smell) and so on. With alliteration and assonance (itself akin to rhyme), rhyme combines to give a music perfectly adapted to the poet's mood and to the idyllic natural scene. It is worth pointing out, though strictly speaking it is assonance more than rhyme that is here involved, that the musically suggestive sound 'lo' occurs eleven times in the last five lines. This is technical virtuosity of a highly self-conscious kind, but it is virtuosity turned to profitable advantage. We shall probably agree that Coleridge would have enjoyed 'The Lotos Eaters', in the light of his dictum: 'the sense of musical delight, with the power of producing it, is a gift of the imagination.'

Donne will provide us with some rhymes used without regard to their intrinsic musical attractiveness, and for a purpose far removed from Tennyson's. These two stanzas are the conclusion of a poem in which he is telling his friend to bring back to him or send him news of the wonders he will encounter on his long travels:

If thou beest borne to strange sights,
  Things invisible to see,
Ride ten thousand dayes and nights,
  Till age snow white haires on thee,
Thou, when thou retorn'st wilt tell mee
All strange wonders that befell thee,
      And sweare
      No where
Lives a woman true, and faire.

If thou findst one, let mee know,
  Such a Pilgrimage were sweet;
Yet do not, I would not goe,
Though at next doore wee might meet,
Though shee were true, when you met her,
And last, till you write your letter,
      Yet shee
      Will bee
False, ere I come, to two, or three.

The poet, in cynical mood – it is not a deep cynicism, he is not so deeply involved, emotionally, as in the sombre 'Nocturnall' stanza previously examined – combines his rhythm with his rhymes into dramatic and meaningful expression; and the parallelism between the two stanzas in tone and rhyming emphasis – they seem to confirm each other – helps considerably in giving the feeling of complete certainty with which he half grimly and half humorously states his conclusion. The first four lines of each stanza are in the nature of introduction to something more significant, and the easy conversational tone has the appropriate unforced rhymes: these spontaneous rhymes are unemphatic because the essential emphasis is to come later, though 'see', 'know', and 'sweet' all have a flavour of amused irony, and 'meet' is a key-word in the imagined situation. Lines five and six in each stanza have a tone of mocking or doubt, to which the double rhymes, with their seemingly off-hand manner, certainly contribute. Then, after these light chatty rhymes, 'tell mee' and 'befell thee', 'met her' and 'letter', in which we can hear Donne's amused and quietly derisive voice, down falls the emphasis with certainty but without violence on the last three lines, in each stanza. The great deliberation of both movement and rhymes gives a sense of finality, of indisputability, to the poet's conclusions. In the first stanza, after the certainty of 'And sweare No where', comes the sting in 'faire': there may be a true woman somewhere, but she is not a beautiful woman; beauty in woman doesn't go with truth. The last three lines of the poem have the same sort of inexorability: 'Yet shee Will be False'; and the very last phrase, just a commonplace colloquial expression, is given a surprising and most effective importance by the comma after 'two', and by the fact that 'three' is the rhyming word; the cynical off-handedness (in this context) of the everyday phrase 'two or three' takes on also the quality of certainty and precision. The poet in his rolé of unromantic worldly-wise-man, by clinching his opinions with such downright speech-rhythms and uncompromising rhymes, has given plausibility to his whole argument and at the same time conveyed the particular quality of his mental-emotional attitude.

Finally, as presenting an example of perfect rhyming in a manner and with an intention very different from Donne's, here is an excerpt from the concluding part of Henry King's 'Exequy' for his dead wife:

> *So close the ground, and 'bout her shade*
> *Black curtains draw, my Bride is laid.*
>
> *Sleep on my Love in thy cold bed*
> *Never to be disquieted!*
> *My last good night! Thou wilt not wake*
> *Till I thy fate shall overtake:*
> *Till age, or grief, or sickness, must*
> *Marry my body to that dust*
> *It so much loves; and fill the room*
> *My heart keeps empty in thy Tomb.*
> *Stay for me there; I will not fail*
> *To meet thee in that hollow Vale.*
> *And think not much of my delay;*
> *I am already on the way,*
> *And follow thee with all the speed*
> *Desire can make, or sorrows breed.*
> *Each minute is a short degree,*
> *And ev'ry houre a step towards thee ...*

'Tis true, with shame and grief I yield,
Thou like the Van first took'st the field,
And gotten hast the victory
In thus adventuring to die
Before me, whose more years might crave
A just precedence in the grave.
But hark! My Pulse like a soft Drum
Beats my approach, tells Thee I come;
And slow howe'er my marches be,
I shall at last sit down by Thee.

The thought of this bids me go on,
And wait my dissolution
With hope and comfort. Dear (forgive
The crime) I am content to live
Divided, with but half a heart,
Till we shall meet and never part.

Almost every rhyming word has significance in that it is associated with one or another of the main thought-feelings of the poem: death and her grave, his desire to follow, his final resignation without despair; and all seem to fall into place inevitably. Nowhere is there any feeling of manufacture or manipulation. One of the essential elements in a full analysis of this poem would be a concern to demonstrate how the rhythm beautifully suggests the inevitability of death, his certainty of his reunion with her in death, and the controlled depth and power of his feeling; and the rhymes, always unostentatious but always helping to shape and give a clarity and edge to the content, to the thought and feeling, coalesce with the rhythm to beat out this steady inevitability. As always in rhyming poetry of high quality there is a point beyond which the discussion of rhyme in isolation from rhythm cannot go. This poem by King would provide an excellent basis for an examination of the integration of rhythm and rhyme. All that will be said here is that the strong, disciplined feeling is felt in the varied but certain progressive beat of the rhythm, and that simultaneously there is the sense of each couplet's being a 'short degree' in the slow march to the consummation.

Chapter 3

IMAGERY

THE use of a merely conventional image in speech or writing – and by image, in this chapter, we mean figure of speech – often has an effect the opposite of what was intended. When you say that somebody was 'as white as a sheet', the staleness of the comparison is apt to cause the statement to pass with very little attention paid to it; in most cases it would be more effective to say 'he was very pale'. A stale and ready-made image is almost invariably evidence of an absence of original first-hand experience in the user, as far as any significance in the phrase itself is intended; it is expression of a loose and general kind, not precise and individual; it doesn't carry in itself any sign of fresh perceptiveness or imagination. It can also detract from the effectiveness of the language around it: if you tack on something like 'it fairly bowled me over' to your narrative of a surprising incident, you are likely to weaken rather than strengthen your effect; the well-worn image *means* so little. Conversely, an image like 'black as the inside of a wolf's throat' is personal in the bad sense; it is rather showy and individualistic, rather 'clever' and affected; images like this, whose validity can't be verified by us because their content is outside our experience – does a wolf's throat suggest blackness particularly even when we try to imagine it? and why a wolf particularly? – tend to take attention *away from* the objects they are supposed to illuminate and make more vivid to our mind and senses.

In a good writer's hands, the image, fresh and vivid, is at its fullest used to intensify, to clarify, to enrich; a successful image helps to make us feel the writer's grasp of the object or situation he is dealing with, gives his grasp of it with precision, vividness, force, economy; and to make such an impact on us, its content, the stuff of which it is made, can't be unduly fantastic and remote from our experience, but must be such that it can be immediately felt by us as belonging in one way or another to the fabric of our own lives. (Familiarity with the content does not of course make the image itself familiar and common; good writers often create surprising images out of the most familiar material.) And as well as having its immediate value, an image may hold within itself something which has associations with other parts of the work to which it belongs – poem or drama or novel; so that its use enhances the complex fullness of the whole. A mature Shakespeare play, for example, is rich in such imagery; in such a play the images are not isolated brilliant units; they have of course their astonishing individual attractiveness, but a complete reading ('complete' meaning 'whole' or 'full') will reveal that they are an inseparable part of the play's total expression.

The aim of the brief examination of the twenty or so images that follow will be to cover the points made in these introductory paragraphs.

When Angus says about Macbeth:

> *Now does he feel*
> *His secret murders sticking on his hands,*

Shakespeare is using a magnificently effective image. The feelings of the tyrant are not referred to with abstract words like 'conscience' or 'guilt' or 'fear', but are given a concrete presentation which powerfully suggests the inescapability of fears and of fate and the resultant terror. The line draws much of its force from the paradox contained in the juxtaposition of the murders' concealment – 'secret' – with the plain and persisting visibility and feeling of the blood on the hands – 'sticking': we are brought very close to a Macbeth who is suffering the terrors of a kind of nightmare; the hands cannot be washed clean, they must betray, and the intended secrecy has turned into its opposite, an overt and palpable presence. The image thus presents an idea or thought in terms of physical sensation, a sensation moreover belonging to the hands, the delicate and sensitive agents of brutal murder: 'now does he *feel*'. Further, it has association with many other lines of the play: Macbeth had previously

feared that his hand would 'The multitudinous seas in-
carnadine, Making the green one red'; and Lady Macbeth
had affirmed, 'A little water clears us of this deed', which
changed later to 'All the perfumes of Arabia will not sweeten
this little hand'. But the lines with which our image has the
strongest affinity are perhaps those in which Lady Macbeth
had urged her husband on: 'But screw your courage to the
sticking place, And we'll not fail'; where the suggestions of
the limit of tension (which the speaker fails to perceive as a
precarious state) of a bow-string and of a musical instru-
ment, and of the dagger (in 'sticking') help to make this
another complex and immediately forceful image. The
point we are concerned with at the moment is the way in
which an image, while having its own 'local' value, may also
recall other key thoughts and feelings and attitudes, and so
add to the strength and complexity of the whole work; it
may confirm, it may ironically recall some previous speech
or action, or modify subtly in some other way. To demonstrate in detail how this occurs in *Macbeth* is of course im-
practicable here – there are factors of plot, themes, character, that would have to be considered – but it can be said
that this correspondence and inter-connexion of images is
evidence both of the poet's grasp of the complexity of the
total situation, and of his integrating power, the power of
organizing complex material into a dramatic whole. In a
real poet's hands, then, such a common word as 'sticking'
can hold great riches.

We do not, of course, expect all images to be rich and
copiously suggestive. The main purpose of an image may be
quite simple, and can be simply fulfilled if there are nn
elements in it positively detracting from the intended effect.
The imagination of Barabas, in Marlowe's *Jew of Malta*,
calls up

> *The wealthy Moor that in the Eastern rocks*
> *Without control can pick his riches up*
> *And in his house heap pearls like pebble-stones;*

and we like the simile suggesting such easy and careless
abundance. We don't demand that the pearls shall be

exactly like pebbles, in colour for instance, or texture; it is the heaping that is the point of the image, and Marlowe makes it 'simply' and adequately: such heaping indicates the easy wealth of the man who 'can pick his riches up' (peculiarly effective in that the glowing vision comes with a colloquial tone and language) and be as careless with pearls as other men are with pebbles underfoot.

In contrast to the concise and suggestive image, there is a kind of loose and diffusive imagery indulged in by some poets for reasons other than those that we have suggested as rightly belonging to it; we might say 'best' instead of 'rightly', for there can be no rules for imagery, but sometimes writers stray too far from what we can justifiably call the essential track. To continue our simple metaphor, they lose their way in making unimportant discoveries. Shelley's famous sequence of similes in his Skylark Ode is inspired by other feelings than a desire to give a vivid impression of the bird; they are explicitly similes – they nearly all begin with 'like' – yet most of them are either vague or inapposite *as comparisons*. They find acceptance, however, with those readers who like to be carried away by the lyrical rush and romantic content of the language; and certainly Shelley's musical verse is often of the kind that almost forces the reader to surrender to the spell of its lyrical onrush. Here is something, not by Shelley, which is similar in its diffusiveness to the 'lark' similes, but far more 'worked' and less impressive as verbal music; Wordsworth is writing about a flower:

> *A nun demure of lowly port;*
> *Or sprightly maiden, of Love's court,*
> *In thy simplicity the sport*
>   *Of all temptations;*
> *A queen in crown of rubies drest;*
> *A starveling in a scanty vest;*
> *Are all, as seems to suit thee best,*
>   *Thy appellations.*

> *A little cyclops, with one eye*
> *Staring to threaten and defy,*
> *That thought comes next – and instantly*
>   *The freak is over,*

The shape will vanish – and behold
A silver shield with boss of gold,
That spreads itself, some faery bold
In fight to cover!

It is doubtful whether anyone reading these lines for the first time would realize that Wordsworth is offering six comparisons for a daisy. Images of this kind obscure the object which they should illuminate. Not one of them is sufficiently precise to be aptly descriptive or suggestive of the daisy only; all of them could as suitably – or unsuitably – be applied to certain other flowers. Working on these lines, a fanciful person could produce a string of such comparisons, which are in general over-ingenious and/or sentimental. For it is only the fancy that is at work, and in these fanciful similes the reality of the flower is wholly lost. The flower is not imaginatively perceived; it is not perceived, for instance, in the way that Wordsworth himself perceived the cuckoo in one of his best-known poems; it is used as the occasion for the manufacture of pretty fancies. And although we are obviously not intended to take this part of the poem very seriously – the poet himself refers to his 'freak' of fancy – we feel that Wordsworth, in offering us such images as a substitute for imagination, is indulging in rather profitless verse-making: the poem has an air of having been written for children, but there is no evidence that the poet had this in mind.

Images manufactured for the sole reason of striking forcibly abound in our poetry. Sometimes they are approvingly called ingenious, sometimes bold; but it can be repeated that what matters most is an image's power to present vividly, suggestively, appositely, and an image fancifully manufactured never does this. Crashaw begins his poem 'Saint Mary Magdalene, or The Weeper', like this:

Hail, sister springs!
Parents of silver-footed rills!
Ever bubbling things!
Thawing crystal! snowy hills,
Still spending, never spent! I mean
Thy fair eyes, sweet Magdalene!

Now whatever suggestions of everlasting purity and 'spiritual refreshment' may be adduced from these images, they are unimpressive because they are so obviously worked. The springs and rills and hills assume an interest of their own quite separate from the eyes of Magdalene; they have too tangible an existence of their own. The images are conceits without imaginative life; the poet cares more about his paradox 'Still spending, never spent', than about the seriousness that he claims for his subject. And later in the same poem, a notorious couplet likens the eyes to:

> *Two walking baths; two weeping motions;*
> *Portable, and compendious oceans,*

and the images are ludicrous because they are tangibly obtrusive. And besides being absurdly hyperbolical in itself, each image is a separate unit, conflicting with its fellows; for the idea of moving water that is common to all of them is treated in such a way as to bring out the ludicrous incongruities. The harmonizing faculty of the imagination, which can reconcile the most diverse elements into a compelling unity, isn't functioning here at all. It is again the 'ingenious', cold fancy, without real feeling behind, that is at work. And even when we try to allow something for the habit or tradition of intermingling the serious and the light that we find in most seventeenth century poetry (frequently a wonderfully successful fusion, where 'serious' and 'light' join to become one in a mature attitude to life), we can feel no more in these lines than the piled-up concoctions of a too palpable fancy.

The imagery of some modern poetry is equally forced. Lines like the following are representative of one 'school' of writers:

> *... Unstable man,*
> *Now bent under the load of his skyscraper grief,*
> *Now spinning joys from the spare pylon's ribs.*

'Skyscraper', intended to suggest greatness of amount, immensity, is altogether inept when coupled with grief: for it is a strong thing, it rises tall, it is distinctly designed: it is

nothing like grief. Moreover, the idea of someone bent
under such a load is certainly a 'staggering' one. The second
line, trotted out to keep the first company, apparently has
some vague reference to wireless. 'Spinning' seems to have
no justification at all. And joys from anything's or anybody's
ribs must be of a strange kind. This imagery is muddled and
meaningless; intended to be striking, it betrays itself as faked.

Some modern poets, rightly looking for imagery, or rather
being ready to find material for imagery, in the things they
see about them in their own time, nevertheless use such
material with startling ineptitude. A good image may
startle too, and unless it is understood it may appear to be
hyperbolical. Even a great critic like Coleridge suggested
'blank height' as the words actually written by Shakespeare,
and not 'blanket', in the line from *Macbeth*: 'Nor heaven
peep through the blanket of the dark.' Coleridge found
something forced and incongruous in the line, and wanted
'blanket' done away with; but the incongruity will be found
to be part of Shakespeare's intention when examination of
the image in its context shows it to be wonderfully apt and
richly suggestive.

An image can possess attractive and interesting qualities
and yet not fulfil the central function of clarifying or illuminating the subject to which it is relevant. Such is the long
simile as used characteristically by Milton and Arnold, who
in illustrating the idea of great bulk, for example, may refer
to the whale and its wanderings in various geographical
environments and to its manner of feeding, with perhaps a
classical or biblical allusion to add to the interest, through
some ten or twelve melodious lines. One of these similes will
be quoted later.

A less obvious example of the type of image that has inter-
est but not complete relevance is this one from Webster's
The White Devil, where Flamineo comments on the Spanish
Ambassador who crosses the stage:

He carries his face in 's ruff, as I have seen a serving-man carry
glasses in a cypress hatband, monstrous steady, for fear of break-
ing; he looks like the claw of a blackbird, first salted, then broiled
in a candle.

These comparisons have a peculiar quality of fantastic vividness; the satirical tone of the first and the macabre content of the second are calculated to raise both amusement and something of a shudder in the audience. They sound well in the mouth of the speaker, who is an observer of manners, cynical, mocking, sententious: wit is expected of him wherever he appears. But his similes will be found to be less impressive, as images, than they may seem to be on their first impact. Their unusual content is interesting, but do we not feel that Flamineo is airing his knowledge and wit rather than describing the Spaniard? Especially is this so in the second. The first certainly does convey a sense of the stiffly held head and rigid bearing of the ambassador, but the 'glasses in a cypress hatband' are rather or quite remote from our experience (though no doubt less so to many of Webster's contemporaries) and so do not register very forcibly. And if we like to be more exacting we can say that Flamineo shouldn't have felt it necessary to go on to explain the point of his comparison; a really forceful image 'explains' itself. However, making fun of the Spaniard was Webster's main concern and no doubt his comparison was much enjoyed. But the matter of the second comparison, stranger and much more remote from common experience than the first, seems introduced only to evoke a kind of thrilled distaste in audience or readers: thrilled because mildly repulsive. The detached claw of a blackbird, subjected to such processes (note that eating seems intended), is in itself sufficiently gruesome for the author's purpose; but as a comparison it fails because we can't even imagine what such a claw, so treated, looks like or tastes like. Nevertheless, if Webster's object was to make the Spaniard appear sinister and unpleasant to the audience, his success was doubtless considerable, especially with the more emotional and less thinking members of it. This second image with its high degree of the fanciful-macabre may be termed successful as far as theatre effect goes; but ultimately it is rather flashily clever, and rootless because it lacks imaginative truth.

Sometimes an image startles with its homeliness. Such an

image will, obviously, come more immediately home to us
than one containing recondite matter. The blackbird's claw
may tickle the fancy strongly, but Macbeth's mind and
hands are immediately present to our senses and our mind.
The commonplace content has of course to be imaginatively
handled to be adequate to the writer's purpose.

When Shelley wrote of Wordsworth that

> *He had as much imagination*
> *As a pint-pot ...*

he used with terseness an image with commonplace content;
but though the material of the image is well known, the
comparison itself is original and surprising. It is predominantly an emotive image; that is to say, we feel it as
an expression of Shelley's inimical feelings towards Wordsworth, and we don't find much exact relevance in it even
though we may know the kind of dullness in Wordsworth
that Shelley was attacking. 'As a pint-pot': it is colloquially
humorous, and startling in its way; but it doesn't carry
much meaning. A pint-pot has just as much and just as
little imagination as any other inanimate object; and if a
pint of imagination is intended it still conveys little or
nothing. A dull, heavy, statically-leaden pot would suit, and
perhaps the poet meant this; but we still feel that the image
has more feeling in it than precise meaning. Its effectiveness
in conveying Shelley's distaste for Wordsworth comes from
a union of the meanness and triviality of the comparison
with the sound and movement of the words: the conception
and sound of 'imagination' is large and expansive, and
when the sudden check comes with the sharp, definite,
scornful sounds 'pint-pot', we feel Shelley's fun and derision
in the anti-climax. As an emotive image then, it is good,
serving Shelley's purpose in suggesting, not explicitly stating, his half-humorous antagonism. But ultimately it is
rather thin in meaning (and after all, a pint-pot has for
many people associations of warm feeling and even of inspiration; we may think of Burns and his 'Inspiring bold
John Barleycorn!'). It is a good example of an image that
makes an immediate impact but which, not being dis-

criminating enough, seems rather too 'smart'; but it is a genuine little *tour de force*. Those who are in agreement with Shelley's opinion probably enjoy the image most. (Incidentally, the criticism in this line and a half does not represent Shelley's whole estimate of Wordsworth; that estimate is often generous.)

An example of the kind of image that has a precise significance and yet is the outcome of strong personal feeling comes in the opening lines of Yeats's 'The Tower':

> *What shall I do with this absurdity –*
> *O heart, O troubled heart – this caricature,*
> *Decrepit age that has been tied to me*
> *As to a dog's tail?*

The simple image, appearing almost to have been slipped in, adds much to the impact of the whole. After the first quiet lines, quiet although 'troubled' – the poet seems to be asking his questions decorously and pathetically – the simile comes out with bitterness and with something of a snarl. The poet's first quiet, reasonable, detached references to 'absurdity' and 'caricature' suddenly turn into absurdity itself, as we see him raging at his helplessness. He sees himself as a grotesque figure, raging impotently, as helpless at the onset of age as a dog raging to escape the tin-can or old kettle tied to his tail. There is the suggestion too that he is reduced to feeling himself to be no more than an animal in creation, subject to the same laws as a dog. The ludicrous picture evoked – Yeats is well aware of course that his protest against nature's law is foolish – and the feeling of futile rage against something not to be shaken off, combine in this 'simple' image with economy and force.

The good writer, it can be repeated, does not use images loosely. His sharp, delicate perceptiveness, and his care to express exactly what he perceives, help to make for him images which have a particular relevance, whether simple or complex. The prose notes of G. M. Hopkins abound with such images:

The next morning a heavy fall of snow. It tufted and toed the firs and yews and went on to load them...

where the simple metaphor 'toed', which is observation and imagination simultaneously – the thing is seen vividly by the poet's eye and by his imaginative mind – exactly describes the effect of the snow in accentuating not only the partly visible roots spreading from the foot of the tree, but also the branches, which in these particular trees often spread like toes and claws. We may consider whether Longfellow had his mind or his eyes on his subject when he wrote this famous quatrain:

> Lives of great men all remind us
> We may make our lives sublime,
> And, departing, leave behind us
> Footprints on the sands of time.

It is probable that the image of the last two lines has been even more instrumental than the sentiment expressed in the whole verse, in making Longfellow a main contributor to autograph albums. For it is a romantically vague and 'mysterious' metaphor. It is a very bad metaphor too. First, sands like these, in their extent and lack of any forward movement, do not in themselves suggest time: surely Longfellow has confusedly in mind the sands of the hour-glass, which do really run, and he hazily and inappropriately introduces footprints. And in any case, he is intending to suggest leaving a lasting name behind, and what is more evanescent than footprints in sand? Also, everybody, the good and the bad, leaves such footprints; they are not reserved as a privilege for those who are inspired by the thought of the 'lives of great men'. The metaphor is no more than a gesture towards solemn impressiveness, and is empty of sensible meaning. It has been popular because, supported by words with an easy emotional appeal content, such as 'sublime', 'departing', 'leave behind us', it has a vague sea-shore mystery or Man Friday atmosphere about it. In a sensible reading the last two lines are immediately felt as bathos. Whatever we think of the sentiment expressed in the first two lines, the image does nothing to support it; in fact, as we perceive the emptiness of the image we are likely to pay the less attention to the sentiment or thought. We are not likely to listen to the moral maxims of an author when we discern such evidence of blurred thinking.

Arising from consideration of Longfellow's metaphor about sand, it is interesting to note certain images of Hopkins and of Marvell. In 'The Wreck of the *Deutschland*', Hopkins writes:

> *I am soft sift*
> *In an hourglass — at the wall*
> *Fast, but mined with a motion, a drift,*
> *And it crowds and it combs to the fall.* ...

This image, though difficult at first to grasp, will be found to succeed where Longfellow's fails: it is apt, precise, and vivid. The process of the sand's sinking in the glass has been observed with delicate accuracy, and the perception is now brought imaginatively into play to present with sensitive exactness a mental-spiritual condition. The motion of the sand powerfully conveys the poet's feeling of an inner weakness and doubt, of a lack of solidity which is undermining him, of a fear of the hastening 'drift' towards failure and dissolution. The weakness is not obviously apparent but it is central and dangerous. Anyone who has stepped on moving sand will have had a frightening feeling of loss of effective action, and there is something of that feeling here. We may think too of the Bible house that was built on sand. The fourth line, the climax of the movement, suggests how inexorably the dissolution proceeds when there is no core of stability. Diction, sound, movement, are of course integral in this superb image, as they are in all richly suggestive images: the image makes us feel sensuously and physically, simultaneously with our grasping the 'intellectual' meaning.

The second image of which Longfellow's can remind us is from Marvell's 'To his Coy Mistress':

> *But at my back I always hear*
> *Time's wingèd chariot hurrying near;*
> *And yonder all before us lie*
> *Deserts of vast eternity.*

And this itself may recall another: set by the side of this Herrick's 'Gather ye rosebuds while ye may, Old Time is still a-flying', and Marvell's distinction will be immediately felt. The comparison is offered here, not just to establish

Marvell's superiority, but to help demonstration. That superiority is in many directions, of which one is the fully realized image. Herrick gives a general and conventional image in conventional terms; Marvell is personally involved in a particular situation, which nevertheless is a representative one for all mankind, and this involvement, the situation being what it is, gives rise to the strong but controlled emotion of his lines. The contrast between the movement and hurry of the life in time, never pausing, and the motionless blank of eternity, is the substance of the vision which, expressed with the peculiar power of the poet's language, conveys this emotion. The vision has a grim quality: the poet is pursued ceaselessly by thoughts of the ever-nearing chariot whose wheels are always audible; there is no escape from the life and laws of time, there is no turning he can take. Ahead, for him (and for everyone), is the stillness, the bareness, the sterility, the dullness, of eternity. The onward movement of life carried compensations of splendour with it – the chariot is 'winged'; static eternity has none. And (paradoxically) the knowledge of those splendours makes his thought the more solemn, and his serious thought makes the splendours appear all the more attractive. Such an account of the material of the image appears clumsily abstract when compared with the poet's swift, 'concretizing' power. Marvell has given emotional significance to the conception of time and eternity, involving all mankind, in a particular, largely visual image. The visual element in the image is emotionally charged, it is inseparable from the moving thought (which the relentless rhythm is part of, too); in the same way, the predominantly tactual image 'sticking on his hands' was seen to make a strong immediate impact and to have rich suggestiveness. (Though not actually relevant to a discussion mainly about imagery, the fruitful use of the word 'all' in Marvell's lines can be noted: it signifies that all the space before us is desert; that this blank eternity is all, there is nothing else; and it is there for all of us.)

The successful development of an image to any considerable length is beyond the capacity of all but the best writers. It requires a sustained pressure of imaginative truth and of intellectual control (these two working as one) if the image is to animate and light up and enrich the theme. Relaxation or carelessness on the writer's part is likely to cause the image to become confused or to disintegrate into meaninglessness or absurdity. The prolonged 'classical' simile has already been instanced as a kind of image in which pointed relevance and intensity are sacrificed to pictorial or melodious qualities; the following, from Arnold's 'Sohrab and Rustum' – it is one of three such images on the same page – is characteristic, and no further comment is necessary here than to say that the simile has content of a thin pictorial interest in itself and that it lacks all appropriateness; the 'As' and the 'so' introduce matters that have only the slightest and most general point of similarity:

> *As some rich woman, on a winter's morn,*
> *Eyes through her silken curtains the poor drudge*
> *Who with numb blacken'd fingers makes her fire –*
> *At cock-crow, on a starlit winter's morn,*
> *When the frost flowers the whiten'd window-panes –*
> *And wonders how she lives, and what the thoughts*
> *Of that poor drudge may be; so Rustum eyed*
> *The unknown adventurous youth, who from afar*
> *Came seeking Rustum, and defying forth*
> *All the most valiant chiefs ...*

The points of *dis*similarity in the comparison are prominent, they almost seem to be emphasized by the poet. And though Arnold was of course well aware of the convention he was writing in, this is no good reason for employing a method the reverse of pointedness and concentration.

One of Arnold's best poems, 'Dover Beach', contains these lines:

> *The Sea of Faith*
> *Was once, too, at the full, and round earth's shore*
> *Lay like the folds of a bright girdle furl'd.*
> *But now I only hear*
> *Its melancholy, long, withdrawing roar,*
> *Retreating, to the breath*
> *Of the night-wind, down the vast edges drear*
> *And naked shingles of the world.*

There is not here the same impression of self-conscious literary manufacture as in the 'Sohrab' excerpt, which was very 'set' and willed into a formal pattern; but the imagery here is not really any more precise and illuminating. Something which once flourished and now is fading is not rightly comparable with the sea at all: the poet's excess of melancholy apparently allows him to conceive of the sea as now ebbing only and as not subject to a recompensing flow. And the simile of the third line belittles and not enhances the idea of a great 'Sea of Faith' by comparing it to something very ordinarily tangible: 'the folds of a bright girdle', especially when 'furl'd', do nothing to suggest the sea's wide and enveloping yet scattered character. 'Bright girdle' seems to be confusedly connected in the poet's mind with the idea of a comforting and protective cloak; which the cold sea is not. The phrase is only a convenient emblem to contrast with the poet's present gloom and so to make it appear the greyer. The last five lines have the impressiveness of its kind of romantic poetry: a certain sonorous music and a vague-mysterious picture and atmosphere. But these qualities are there for emotive purposes only: Arnold is indulging in his sadness and he intends us to indulge too; he frankly describes a scene in such a way as to lull us into accepting it (does it competently too, if without great distinction), forgetting that it is a 'Sea of Faith' he is dealing with. The actual sea's sounds and shores engross him, and the image has in fact vanished; and the result is strange: for instead of deploring the disappearance of Faith, which was really Arnold's theme, we find ourselves enjoying a description of the sea. The failure of the imagination and intellect to create and control effective imagery is common in Victorian poetry generally.

As Arnold will cajole many readers by his substitution of romantic pictorial and melodious appeal for the meaningful sharpness and fertility of good imagery, so Browning sometimes impresses the unalert with an air of dramatic sprightliness, a sprightliness which, when analysed, will often be found to cover confused thinking. In the extract that follows he is expressing his sense of his life's struggle and search for an ideal love that seems always to be eluding him:

> Escape me?
> Never —
> Beloved!
> While I am I, and you are you,
>   So long as the world contains us both,
>   Me the loving and you the loth,
> While the one eludes, must the other pursue.
> My life is a fault at last, I fear —
>   It seems too much like a fate indeed!
>   Though I do my best I shall scarce succeed —
> But what if I fail of my purpose here?
>
> It is but to keep the nerves at strain,
>   To dry one's eyes and laugh at a fall,
> And baffled, get up to begin again —
>   So the chase takes up one's life, that's all.
> While, look but once from your farthest bound,
>   At me so deep in the dust and dark,
> No sooner the old hope drops to the ground
>   Than a new one, straight to the self-same mark,
>   I shape me —
>   Ever
>   Removed!

It is the imagery of the second verse with which we are here concerned. Life interpreted as a chase could be a good basis for an image; but in Browning's lines the chase, the difficult journey, becomes a rather melodramatic *tour de force* in itself. The purpose of his image is twofold: first it gives the general setbacks of the journey, then it refers to the failure of his positive hopes; and here again the ideas have possibilities. But the first four lines are nearly all cliché; this sort of journey with its difficulties and its come-up-smiling moral has been undertaken in literature so many times. And do the images of drying eyes and laughing at falls do anything to suggest an adult feeling of life's recurring disappointments? The child who has tumbled down and who is told to be brave is far too simple a parallel. Also, lines two and three being apparently a description of one happening, the parts composing it are given in the wrong order; this inaccuracy may seem a little thing, but it does show that the thought under the image is loose, and after all Browning is trying to persuade us of the significance of the stages of his journey. This lack of real interest in the work and worth of the image, due partly to loose thought and partly no doubt to putting the requirements of the rhyme-scheme first, betrays a certain shallowness and vagueness of emotion. In the second part of the image, the poet represents his hopes by arrows: apart from the doubtful appropriateness of representing the forming of new hopes and their dissolution by such a mechanically swift process as the poet offers us, there is a melodramatic element which is enough in itself to invalidate the image; in line six, for instance, largely for the sake of some intended-impressive alliteration, the poet becomes a ludicrous figure toiling through deep dust and aiming his arrows ineffectively one after another, and seeing them drop to ground in the dark; and the mark at which he aims the sharp, killing arrow is the lover-ideal, though he knows apparently, by the last two lines, that he can never hit it. The whole verse can be accepted as an adequate expression of frustration and effort only by those who let themselves be overcome by the rather cheap feeling conveyed in a jaunty rhythm. The truth is that Browning has manufactured a situation to exhibit his resilience in adverse circumstances; and it is, in the main, the showy, melodramatic, and jumbled imagery that gives him away. (How conscious Browning was of such manufacture it would be hard to say; it seems obvious that there is a good deal of self-deception in the poem, though the experience given in it had its origin, no doubt, in some kind of genuine personal feeling. It is in the attempted development and elaboration of the feeling that the poem becomes a muddle: the facts or situation that prompted the poem have been grossly 'poeticized'.)

The effectual use of imagery through a prolonged passage may be illustrated in this extract from 'The Waste Land':

Here is no water but only rock
Rock and no water and the sandy road
The road winding above among the mountains
Which are mountains of rock without water
If there were water we should stop and drink
Amongst the rock one cannot stop or think
Sweat is dry and feet are in the sand
If there were only water amongst the rock
Dead mountain mouth of carious teeth that cannot spit
Here one can neither stand nor lie nor sit
There is not even silence in the mountains
But dry sterile thunder without rain
There is not even solitude in the mountains
But red sullen faces sneer and snarl
From the doors of mudcracked houses
                                    If there were water

And no rock
If there were rock
And also water
And water
A spring
A pool among the rock
If there were the sound of water only
Not the cicada
And dry grass singing
But sound of water over a rock
Where the hermit-thrush sings in the pine trees
Drip drop drip drop drop drop drop
But there is no water.

The immediate occasion is, as Mr Eliot indicates in a note, Christ's journey to Emmaus after the Resurrection; but the essential significance lies in its being also a journey through the Waste Land, the modern world as perceived by the poet. What the passage demonstrates among other things is a superb use of a number of simple images, all closely related. For the images in themselves really are simple – rock, water, sand, bird-song – and there is no attempt at complex development of any one of them. But out of the simple material the poet creates his landscape which is the embodiment of the feeling of barrenness, longing, weariness. Some readers might prefer to say that what we are dealing with here is symbolism rather than imagery; and certainly the images, excepting the 'Dead mountain mouth of carious teeth', are not of the manifest kind that we have been examining. But they are present, not as explicit comparisons but as comparisons implied and incorporated in the setting and spiritual atmosphere. The passage can be regarded as one long metaphor. In a full analysis it would be shown how the imagery is inseparable from the rhythm, and how suggestive this rhythm is, with its levels of weary monotony alternating with movements towards life when spring or pool or sound of water is longed for, and falling back into 'defeat' again at the end: it would be shown how the 'monotony' goes with a subtly varied movement which is the reverse of the monotonous as exemplified in Poe's 'Raven' manner. The echoes and repetitions, the alternations of rock and water, in this weary and yet strong and controlled rhythm, convey the very feeling of spiritual drouth. There are of course Biblical associations: the Lord who brought water out of the rock of flint; the cicada, the 'burden' of the grasshopper in Ecclesiastes. And these are parts of a total nightmarish vision – nightmarish because true and plain to the poet – where rock is barren and cannot flow with the waters of grace and health and faith; where the sandy road is hot and dry and leads to sterility; where the sweat of effort dries uselessly; where 'feet are in the sand', laborious, unfirm, and out of contact with the moist life-giving soil; where even silence and solitude are prevented by the noise of fruitless toil and the evidences of human strife. The desire for the 'waters of healing' is deeply felt in the contrast of the spring and the pool and the dripping-water song of the bird in the sweet-smelling pines with the dry rasp of the cicada and the singing (!) of the withered grass and especially with the 'dead mountain mouth'. The line containing this last image, evoking the horror of decay and dryness and lack of relief, owes much of its effect to the quiet and matter-of-fact way in which it, so horrible in itself, takes its place among the others. It also brings horribly close the identification of this physical setting with the spiritual condition of humanity. But finally it is the cumulative effect rather than the salience of individual elements that is so impressive; the poet's truth and consistencey of feeling move him to bring together his separate, and in the main simple, images to create an emotionally and imaginatively coherent total impression.

The section can be closed with a good and clear example of the development, with relevance, of an image; Angelo, the acting civic head of Vienna, in *Measure for Measure*, is speaking to Escalus:

> *We must not make a scarecrow of the law,*
> *Setting it up to fear the birds of prey,*
> *And let it keep one shape, till custom make it*
> *Their perch, and not their terror.*

The matter of the image is simple and familiar, everyone knows the scarecrow; but the poet's handling makes it into something new. The old-age figure of the countryside is used to bring home with economy and clarity the significance of the thought. Angelo is stressing the importance of the law's enforcement; if not enforced it is as mockable as a scarecrow. If the law is not shown to be alive in its working, if it is only a dead form, it is no more useful than a scarecrow that has been recognized by the birds as a form without life. As the birds prey on the land, so do lawbreakers on city or state. Shakespeare, always aware of the possible value of ambiguity in words, skilfully uses 'fear' both with its Elizabethan active meaning of 'frighten' and with its ordinary passive meaning indicating that the law fears the lawbreakers; the farmer fears the birds, and sets up the scarecrow to 'fear' them away. If the law is a lifeless formality, set into a shape known by all to be lifeless, the lawbreakers will lose all fear of it, will mock it and will even make positive use of it. This image is perhaps not so richly imaginative and suggestive as some of the others we have examined; but it is vividly apt, clear, and exact in its application, and as such is characteristic of the 'precise' Lord Angelo's thought. It also clearly illustrates a factor that makes for great effectiveness in imagery: namely, the juxtaposition in an image of things which ordinarily are not

associated with one another. Here, the association of the
formal, august, and normally feared law with the unkempt,
bizarre, half loved and half contemned scarecrow, helps to
give the image its sharp impact. (In its context the image is
the more significant as belonging to Angelo, whose lack of
warmth and of human friendliness makes us feel that he has
an aloof, hard superiority to the humble scarecrow.)
Similar associations could be examined in several of our
other images – Yeats's 'Decrepit age' and 'dog's tail', for
instance, and that 'mountain mouth', in the landscape of
the Waste Land, 'that cannot spit'; the conjunction of such
diverse things or ideas in one idea or perception is often the
source of the surprising or shocking force of a good image.
Such a conjunction shows the writer's power of assimilating
different kinds of experience, and this helps him to fuse his
sense-perceptions, his emotion and his thought into an
organic expression.

Chapter 4

POETIC THOUGHT

THE main endeavours of this section will be to distinguish
between the presence of thought in poetry as an activity
helping to shape the whole expression, and the presence of
'thoughts' or ideas or concepts merely as part of the subject
matter or as ends or near-ends in themselves; to show that
a poet dealing with thoughts is not necessarily a strong-
thinking poet; and to indicate that what we understand by
poetic thought, at its finest, is fused with feeling and
sensuous perceptiveness. This last point has perhaps already
to some extent made itself felt in our examination of
imagery.

Writing of any kind demands some thought; it is impossible to write the simplest sentence for ourselves without
some thought. But the thought which matters beyond
utilitarian and social considerations (such as that which
occurs in most of the letters we write, the newspapers we
read), is that which comes home to us with a certain force,
which has its own profundity or subtlety; this kind of
thought has qualities that make it more than an exposition
of subject matter. Subtlety: the word as used above prompts
a warning. An author can fill his pages with the most
abstruse thoughts and yet not be impressive as an individual
writer; he may be even naïve as a thinker. Argumentation is
not necessarily individual thinking. Thoughts and ideas,
often culled from other writers and thinkers – religious,
political, philosophical, economic, sociological, psychological and so on – abound in the pages of many modern
novelists; such thoughts can valuably stimulate of course,
and increase our knowledge. But unless thought is an integral part of the novelist's sensibility, that is to say if his
thoughts and ideas are not an integral part of the organic
whole of his work, having their roots in his own experience,
his own living, they are likely to become no more than an

exhibition, clever maybe and even brilliant, of his mental goods. In a novel of Aldous Huxley there are many ideas; it is obvious also that the author has himself thought a good deal about life. But the overwhelming impression that we get from his work is that the author has gathered together a vast stock of miscellaneous information and ideas from books, and that the use he makes of them gives his novels sometimes an air of greater understanding and comprehensiveness than his own experience of life can supply.

A good novelist often makes us feel the power of his thought when it is linked with and follows inevitably upon his presentment of people and events, setting and atmosphere. When George Eliot wishes to express the 'idea' of ignorance and shallow insular pride, she doesn't merely make abstract statements or asseverations; she shows us the encounter of Mr Bult and Herr Klesmer (in *Daniel Dronda*), which in its vivid truth of concrete detail is immediately impressive; the 'thought', the insight giving rise to the thought, are there in her presentment of the actions and gestures and speeches. She can and does add comments when by doing so she can reveal the more fully her understanding and grasp of the situation; but the powerful basis of the thought is in the concrete presentment. The idea of complacent superiority with ignorance is *felt* through the actions and words of Mr Bult; we feel the thought of George Eliot here as we feel poetic thought.

It shouldn't be necessary to say (it wouldn't be if there were not so many people who judged the value of literature according to its confirmation of or antagonism to their own ideas and opinions), that we can feel and appreciate the impact of a writer's thought without necessarily taking up his 'doctrinal' position. We can enjoy the poetry of Hopkins without being Roman Catholics; and we don't have to be dissenters before we can enjoy Marvell. Different men can hold different doctrines with equal sincerity and fervour. Hopkins and Marvell have different religions as far as doctrine is concerned; they are the same in having an individual and sensitive apprehension of life and a technique adequate to express it. One of the best things that literature can do for us is to teach us the possibility of sincerity in those who have beliefs different from our own, making clear to us the unwisdom of attaching ourselves over-rigorously to 'final conclusions'. The greatness of Hopkins and Marvell – many more names could be instanced – does not depend on the positions they found themselves impelled to take up in religion and politics.

The kind of thought manifested by George Eliot, a prose writer, as discussed above, is closely akin to poetic thought. It isn't simply *stated*; it has a living embodiment and force in dialogue, action, situation, gesture. And this kind of living thought is present (not continuously, of course), and is manifested in a variety of ways, in all good writers. But for the purpose of clarity and economy of demonstration, conforming with the scope of the book, this section will deal henceforth with poetry only.

> *Nature shews a forest to you,*
> *And Man his carved cathedrals fine;*
> *To which, do you think, is more homage due:*
> *To human effort, or ease divine?*

This anonymous quatrain states two obvious factual truths (though 'fine' indicates a point of view as well, an attitude towards the fact), and asks one question. It is a question intended to make us think; but the lines themselves haven't the quality that we call poetic thought. For they are too explicit, they are only the versified expression of an idea mentally conceived. The idea itself could prompt a discussion, a debate, though our own thought straightway may tell us that there is little point in setting one manifestation of beauty against another merely for argument's sake. The 'do you think' of the author sounds somewhat timid and tentative too, as if he half recognizes the needlessness of his question. But beyond the point of the idea itself, which strictly is not the object of our examination, we may ask whether we feel the author to have been *impelled* to put the thought into verse, for the verse has a rather flat movement and a rather too set, too neat pattern. The verse is not at all pre-

tentious, however; it has the considerable 'negative' virtue
of not trying to impress showily, it is 'sincere', without being
forceful. In so far as memorability is desirable it may pass
like 'Thirty days hath September', though this last has of
course its practical usefulness too. But as *poetic* thought the
lines may be said to fail in that they are too general;
language is being used only as a convenient *vehicle* for the
'thought', not as the one indispensable means of enforcing
vividly a 'thought' which the author has vividly experienced.
(What we mean by 'experiencing a thought' will be made
clearer as the section proceeds.)

Nearer to poetic thought are the famous lines of Lovelace:

> *Stone walls do not a prison make,*
> *Nor iron bars a cage;*
> *Minds innocent and quiet take*
> *That for a hermitage.*

Nearer, but still not fulfilling all we expect if we have en-
countered poetic thought at its finest. What the lines do,
especially the first two, is to give picturesque-metaphorical
expression to the idea of the mind's freedom. They function
in much the same way as many proverbs: 'Empty vessels
make the most noise', or 'Make hay while the sun shines'.
Lovelace advances his proposition neatly and with an
accomplished touch; he skilfully emphasizes most of his
important words: the sound of 'stone walls' is solid, the 'iron
bars' are hard and strong; 'Minds' receives its due weight
in the proposition, as the essential contrast with the tangible
substances. The acceptability of the idea is not at stake; we
shall probably agree in accepting it as a half-truth at most.
The author is stating, not arguing. And what has given the
verse its popularity is the paradoxical nature of the statement: because stone walls *do* a prison make. So the lines
appear as insightful and striking, as many paradoxes do.
The idea is not a new one: 'I could be bounded in a nutshell
and count myself a king of infinite space ...' says Hamlet.
But again, the newness of the idea is not at stake. What we
are seeking is poetic thought, and this is not dependent on

the newness of the idea (how frequent are really new ideas?),
but on the writer's power to use words to convey in the
fullest degree what he has 'thought feelingly'. There is a
rather brittle assertiveness about Lovelace's neatly balanced
lines; we feel that someone else could have suggested the
idea to him (though in fact no-one did) so that he could
give it a neat and attractive form. In finer writing, idea and
words are one: there is less the sense of a cleverly expressed
idea that was already present as an idea *before* being expressed in language, than of the writer's *creating* his meaning as he proceeds; less a sense of formulation than of progressive creation.

Gray's 'Elegy' contains many 'thoughts'; here is one of
the finest stanzas:

> *Full many a gem of purest ray serene*
> *The dark unfathom'd caves of ocean bear;*
> *Full many a flower is born to blush unseen,*
> *And waste its sweetness on the desert air.*

Without a knowledge of what the rest of the poem says, we
should still immediately know that these lines are metaphorical, that the idea is that of unrecognized or unknown
beauty or unrealized capacities; the poet does succeed in
conveying the idea, he is as far from banal expression of a
commonplace as he may well be. If we believed that the
function of poetry *par excellence* was to clothe 'thoughts' in
'beautiful' dress, these lines would be hard to better. And in
any case they have their own distinguished quality: the
unforced, measured movement is used admirably to carry
the feeling of melancholy that goes with the thought; and
this steady movement makes at least partly acceptable the
idealization in Gray's chosen symbols of hidden value; for
they *are* idealized, these pure gems and the blushing
flowers, as soon as we think of the human analogy implied
in them. We may partly accept them for their intrinsic
attractiveness, but nowhere are we *compelled* by the thought.
We could question the rightness of 'blush unseen' – a key
phrase from the standpoint of the thought – as being
touched with sentimental humanizing. But we hardly care

to be so exacting here, for we feel that Gray himself is not deeply concerned, either emotionally or intellectually, with the thought. What he is most concerned with, we feel, is to suggest the beauty of the contrast of clear gem with dark under-ocean caves, and to express musically his sense of the transient sweetness of the unknown flower. His appeal is really to the romantic fancy and to the ear. For the sake of the romantic suggestiveness and the beauty of the sound (those who look for vowel-music in poetry have a feast here; and note how the sounding and resonant heaviness of the second line contrasts with the soft openness of the last – Tennyson never bettered effects like these), we accept the fact that the idea is twice given. (There doesn't seem so much justification for the repetition in the Lovelace, where the second line says exactly the same as the first.) What is not felt in Gray, however – and in this he is like Lovelace – is the presence of vital poetic thought as a shaping factor of the whole expression. He is giving a colourful illustration of a popular-democratic idea: musical, dignified, romantically attractive, the lines have little cogency or power as an expression of a 'truth' personally arrived at.

The following lines of Hopkins, once their apparent strangeness has been recognized as the genuine personal experience that it is ('strangeness' because Hopkins is still little known), will demonstrate a way of the functioning of words radically different from that of any we have so far considered in this section. They are the beginning of a poem having as theme the transience or seeming transience of beauty, and called 'The Leaden Echo and the Golden Echo':

> *How to keep – is there any any, is there none such, nowhere known some,*
> *bow or brooch or braid or brace, lace, latch or catch or key to keep*
> *Back beauty, keep it, beauty, beauty, beauty ... from vanishing away?*

These lines are chosen expressly as a conveniently strong contrast to those of Lovelace and Gray, and as a clear and simple exemplification of the working of poetic thought. The thought itself is simple too, and is as common a thought as can be found in literature. But the poet's way of apprehending it is individual, and the 'thinking' is strong. By the way in which he uses language we feel the urgency of the thought, the importance it has for him personally; he is deeply involved in it. He doesn't make neat or solemnly impressive versified propositions; he conveys his thought in an almost physically felt effort to find a way to save beauty from vanishing. Full analysis would reveal the rhythmically forceful adaptation of the inflexions of the speaking voice, the stresses and pauses being used to convey the longing and near-despair of the writer; it would examine the sources of the effective contrast in movement and sound, corresponding to the difference in content, between the two lines, the first with its searching and repeated phrases and almost desperately listed short and definite fastening and holding contrivances, the second, after the opening words, diminishing and fading 'away' with an effect similar to that of 'Are melted into air, into thin air'. The words themselves function strongly, they are not simply a vehicle for the thought and they do not colourfully *illustrate* a thought; if the words were altered even slightly, we should lose the quality of *individuality* in the poet's thought. The choice of the objects in the first line (all ineffectual ultimately, whether strong or beautiful in themselves) shows thought, but it is mainly in their order-arrangement, with the alliteration and assonance functioning sharply and then passing into the dying-away second line, that poetic thought is felt. (In spite of its initial strangeness for many readers, this extract shows poetic thought functioning comparatively simply; it is not richly complex as the finest of Hopkins is.) Poetic thought occurs when the idea is felt, not merely utilized, by the poet, who makes his words unfold the thought as it develops; usually, the thought is felt through concrete words and images, the abstract being too vague and general. A comment by Hopkins on these two lines of his is interesting; he is writing to Robert Bridges: 'You must know that words like "charm" and "enchantment" will not do. ... "Back" is not pretty, but it gives that feeling of physical constraint which I want.'

A consideration of three complete short poems will help

to clarify further this rather elusive subject of poetic thought. Here is one of the 'In Memoriam' poems:

Ring out, wild bells, to the wild sky,
     The flying cloud, the frosty light:
     The year is dying in the night;
Ring out, wild bells, and let him die.

Ring out the old, ring in the new,
     Ring, happy bells, across the snow:
     The year is going, let him go;
Ring out the false, ring in the true.

Ring out the grief that saps the mind,
     For those that here we see no more;
     Ring out the feud of rich and poor,
Ring in redress to all mankind.

Ring out a slowly dying cause,
     And ancient forms of party strife;
     Ring in the nobler modes of life,
With sweeter manners, purer laws.

Ring out the want, the care, the sin,
     The faithless coldness of the times;
     Ring out, ring out my mournful rhymes,
But ring the fuller minstrel in.

Ring out false pride in place and blood,
     The civic slander and the spite;
     Ring in the love of truth and right,
Ring in the common love of good.

Ring out old shapes of foul disease;
     Ring out the narrowing lust of gold;
     Ring out the thousand wars of old,
Ring in the thousand years of peace.

Ring in the valiant man and free,
     The larger heart, the kindlier hand;
     Ring out the darkness of the land,
Ring in the Christ that is to be.

The idea on which this poem is built up – the ringing in of good and the ringing out of evil – has certainly been en-

larged and elaborated by a kind of thinking; but it is thinking of the kind which takes a number of ready-made concepts or thoughts and manipulates them to fit into a set
moral scheme expressed in a regular verbal pattern. The
admirers of this poem – it is a popular one – could say of
course that the author had here no intention of exhibiting
thought-processes of any significance; and they might perhaps defend the mechanical quality of his antitheses by
declaring a purposed simplicity. But the enumeration of a
string of what turn out to be mostly clichés is little guarantee
of the moral feeling which we are meant to accept as the
inspiration of the poem; and it is a poem which ultimately
stands or falls by the genuineness of its proclaimed moral
attitude. A more deeply 'thoughtful' poet would not have
been so mechanically fluent in his balanced phrasings: what
we have here is more a willed arrangement than a development. Tennyson has made use of twenty or more 'thoughts'
or ideas but has not shaped them into anything organically
impressive. The thoughts are brought in 'from the outside',
from the general stock of thoughts, and are then made sub-
servient to the pre-ordained form of the poem. Conse-
quently there is something of a jumble; there does not seem
to have been even a conscious mental effort to give the
thoughts a significant order. Perhaps the poet tried to put
too many diverse ideas into the poem; the attempt to include
so much results in a concentration on nothing; and without
questioning the genuineness of Tennyson's desire to see good
triumphant, we can't but feel that he has here allowed the
declaiming manner of the skilful public bard to take precedence over the deepest personal thinking of Tennyson the
man. Real feeling would have meant more concentrated
thought, an absence of or fewer clichés, and a less mechanical pattern.

The second of our complete poems is by Thomas Hardy;
it is entitled 'The Sleep-Worker':

> *When wilt thou wake, O Mother, wake and see –*
> *As one who, held in trance, has laboured long*
> *By vacant rote and prepossession strong –*
> *The coils that thou hast wrought unwittingly;*

Wherein have place, unrealized by thee,
Fair growths, foul cankers, right enmeshed with wrong,
Strange orchestras of victim-shriek and song,
And curious blends of ache and ecstasy? –

Should that morn come, and show thy opened eyes
All that Life's palpitating tissues feel,
How wilt thou bear thyself in thy surprise? –

Wilt thou destroy, in one wild shock of shame,
Thy whole high heaving firmamental frame,
Or patiently adjust, amend, and heal?

A summary of the prose-meaning is enough to reveal that there is in this poem a way of thinking very different from that in the Tennyson. Hardy is characteristically questioning the nature of the divine government of the world: it seems to him that of a Being who, as in an unseeing and unknowing trance, has for ages ruled with a meaningless and repetitive routine of law (vacant rote), and with a strong bent in one direction (prepossession strong); he asks when this Being will awake to the unsatisfactory tangle of life on earth, and whether It will then in shame destroy everything or begin a transformation into something finer. There can be no argument about the presence of a positive kind of thought in this poem; whatever we think of the 'rightness' of the thought, of the desirability or otherwise of its acceptance, of its 'originality' or otherwise, it is clear that the poet has speculated seriously about life. Instead of a number of the stock ideas and phrases of the kind that were in evidence in Tennyson's poem, and that were given there in a rather perfunctory manner and in an un-significant order, we have in Hardy one main idea, combining question and statement, developed steadily to the final, important word, 'heal'. There are only three sentences in the poem, the first covering the whole of the octet: this explains why the poet feels he must address and question the great 'Mother'. The second asks 'how', following the 'when' of the first; and the third suggests possible answers to the 'how'. There is, then, a progression in thought; and the steady movement of the verse helps to convey the serious, inquiring, and rather grim quality of this thought. We feel too, behind the poem as it were, a sympathy for human suffering: 'Life's palpitating tissues', and the 'shock of shame' that the Creator should feel on awakening to the truth. But – and here we really come to the object of our present inquiry – the language of the poem reveals, despite the presence of the kind of sensitiveness referred to above, that Hardy's feeling has been heavily overlaid by his speculation: his thought is sincere in that it is conscientiously worked out, and it is inspired by sympathy, but it lacks the direct and immediate impressiveness of 'true' poetic thought. It is more like thought in the ordinary sense; that is, speculation, pondering. It deals mainly with what are large abstractions, notwithstanding the novelty of some of the phrasing: 'coils', 'fair growths', 'right enmeshed with wrong', 'strange orchestras ...', 'curious blends', 'palpitating tissues' – nothing makes a sharp, particular impact; and there is a certain amount of repetition which might profitably have been avoided, such as line eight after line seven; and of straining after impressive bigness as in expressions like 'coils that thou hast wrought', 'strange orchestras of victim-shriek and song', 'one wild shock of shame', 'whole high heaving firmamental frame': though in this last instance we may admire, despite the melodramatic tone, the way in which the rising movement is set off against the slow, quiet, and deliberate last line. Speculation about 'The Sleep-Worker' perhaps asks for expression in slow, solemn lines; but Hardy's language doesn't really do much to bring the thought home. It is felt to be over-thorough, hence laboured; it unfolds the content of a thought, but it hasn't the active, lithe, functioning quality of language which goes with fine emotional and imaginative perceptiveness in the creation of poetic thought. His words *refer to* rather than *act*; they are not *alive* enough to satisfy fully. The lines below are given to demonstrate the kind of vividness and life that Hardy's lacks. Where Hardy rather cumbrously displays his thought, sincere and personal as it is, Shakespeare's thought is felt in and through the strong, definite, and vivid images; and their impact does not come only from their intrinsic suggestiveness; it is the stronger because of their inevitable-seeming 'at-oneness' with the strong and flexible speech-rhythms. The lines could well be made the ground for a full discussion on poetic thought, but they are offered here mainly as a foil to the mode of thought in Hardy's poem. A point that can be profitably stressed is the great force that the concrete-poetic can carry as against the prose-abstract: instead of 'the rich in authority are in a position to pass judgement, though they may be greater sinners, on the poorer petty law-breakers', the poet says 'the usurer hangs the cozener'. The lines are from *King Lear*:

> *The usurer hangs the cozener.*
> *Through tatter'd clothes small vices do appear;*
> *Robes and furr'd gowns hide all. Plate sin with gold,*
> *And the strong lance of justice hurtless breaks;*
> *Arm it in rags, a pigmy's straw does pierce it.*

Yeats's 'Death' is the third of the complete poems under immediate consideration:

> *Nor dread nor hope attend*
> *A dying animal;*
> *A man awaits his end*
> *Dreading and hoping all;*
> *Many times he died,*
> *Many times rose again.*
> *A great man in his pride*
> *Confronting murderous men*
> *Casts derision upon*
> *Supersession of breath;*
> *He knows death to the bone —*
> *Man has created death.*

This short, strong poem has at least five 'thoughts', all significant in any serious contemplation of the poet's theme. All the thoughts are given explicit utterance; they are declared statements, they are not contained or potently implied and suggested in images. To have made a poem out of propositions, stated with such bareness, is Yeats's triumph. Perhaps that is not perfectly accurate, for the poem doesn't exist for the propositions merely; we don't feel that

the poem sprang from 'ideation' at all; although the poem
is in a sense made of thought and thoughts, and although
the thoughts are in themselves significant, it is the presence
of something else that gives the deep impressiveness and that
makes us feel we are in contact with a kind of poetic thought
and not merely with stated, general ideas. The presence is
that of the poet's feeling, almost of his character, and this is
most powerfully felt in the rhythmical firmness and certainty; a rhythm which, though possessing a certain stark-
ness appropriate to the unelaborated and uncompromising
thought, is sinewy and never brittle. The words are in the
main solid-sounding, and are most economically used; not a
word is superfluous, and it is probable that not one could
be altered without impairing the whole. They are those of a
man with his mind intent on his subject, of a strongly disciplined poet. At the heart of the poem is the feeling which
with Yeats goes with the idea of the great man 'confronting'
– strong, physical word – his enemies, the 'murderous men'
for whom the poet feels and makes us feel derision; we feel
his own scorn for them. The juxtaposition of 'Supersession
of breath', diminishing death's importance, and 'He knows
death to the bone', with its powerful certainty of the man's
courage in knowledge, is extremely effective: death is belittled not only by the euphemistic way of describing it in
'Supersession of breath', but also in the very sound of the
phrase depending so much on movement of the lips; the
phrase is finely suggestive of lack of solidity, and it is set off
by, as it in turn sets off, the firm roundness and hard certainty of 'He knows death to the bone', where the sound and
movement present decision and character. The juxtaposition leads into the truth, paradoxical to 'normal opinion', of the last line: the profound truth that death is not the
antithesis of life but a part of it; man has mentally created
death, for animals it doesn't exist. The conclusion, in both
senses of the word, has been reached by successive stages and
takes us back to the beginning again; it is unquestionably
'true' in the sense that the statements whose truth might be
debated by abstract thinkers have here that kind of logic
and belief which have their origin in emotion and thought.

What would have been a series of staccato assertions in the hands of a lesser poet is here a consecutive whole, bound together by the assured, individual movement and tone which spring from and contain the poet's stoic strength. And though the poem does not exhibit poetic thought at its most vivid – the stoic attitude isn't conducive to immersion in all the varied and rich complexities of living – the propositions have an emotional validity and so are an integral part of the total poetic effect.

The mere advancement of ideas in verse form is not thoughtful poetry; this would appear, then, to be obvious enough. Yet considerable and even great poets have on occasion so far been untrue to themselves as to give wordy utterance to their favourite ideas and opinions and to count this as poetry. Milton's dictum about poetry's needing to be 'simple, sensuous and passionate', is rather arbitrary, but if we construe 'simple' as 'not needlessly elaborate' we shall find that much fine poetry will conform to it. If he had always heeded it himself he would have produced less of the kind of mere argumentation in verse that justified Pope's comment on this particular element in 'Paradise Lost': 'In Quibbles Angel and Archangel join, And God the Father turns a School-divine'. Wordsworth too, is notoriously prone to philosophize prosily in blank verse. His 'philosophy', his thoughts about and his attitude to life, as embedded in his finest poetry, are of great value and beauty, but it is far less convincing when it is given utterance like this:

> *There are in our existence spots of time*
> *That with distinct pre-eminence retain*
> *A renovating virtue, whence – depressed*
> *By false opinion and contentious thought,*
> *Or ought of heavier or more deadly weight,*
> *In trivial occupations, and the round*
> *Of ordinary intercourse – our minds*
> *Are nourished and invisibly repaired ...*

The content of the statement propounded here, that there are moments of our lives which, when we recollect them in times of hopelessness and weariness, will relieve and sustain us, commands a wide measure of assent. But though we may agree with our 'mental' mind, we are not impelled to believe in the way that a more concrete expression could impel us; the writing is not sufficiently 'simple, sensuous, and passionate' to move us in that way. The passage states with large abstractions; the words are only used as servants of the idea; the philosophy is first, the poetry a poor second. Where general and abstract thought predominates, the essential poetic quality is lacking: that is, the alive and enlivening individual sensibility which grasps and presents the thought with vitality. The expression here has the mark of a serious 'thinking' mind and it exhibits a certain skill in managing a long sentence, but it is heavy and has no individual sharpness. (The fact that the lines are a sort of introduction to a narrative of a childhood incident doesn't affect our judgement of their poetic value.) In much of his early work Wordsworth gives experiences which were peculiarly his own; their significance was perceived and expressed with an extraordinarily personal insight and freshness. In such work we see, hear, touch, we are given perceptiveness as we read; and to accept the 'conclusions' is a part of our whole response because they are an integral part of the poet's experience. The poet's sensuous and spiritual experience is incarnated, given 'body', in the poetry; the reality of the experience makes it irrelevant to extract 'thoughts' and give them consideration in isolation. In the lines that we have quoted, Wordsworth is giving undue and over-impressive importance to an idea that he has extracted and isolated from his full experience.

Donne and Dryden and others have reasoned and argued admirably in verse. Mr Eliot has expressed profound and far-reaching thoughts in the 'Four Quartets' and elsewhere. But in Donne and Dryden there are qualities that matter more than the 'truth' of the thoughts; and Mr Eliot's verse, seeming to follow thought and so presenting the very movement of thought with all the accompanying nuances of feeling and attitude, is as subtle as the thought itself and has been inseparably created with it.

A passage from Dryden's 'Religio Laici', where the poet

is referring to the efforts of ancient philosophers to find answers to the 'riddle' of existence, will show how attractive the verse of exposition, reasoning, and inquiry can be:

> As blindly groped they for a future state,
> And rashly judged of Providence and Fate.
> But least of all could their endeavours find
> What most concerned the good of human kind;
> For Happiness was never to be found,
> But vanished from them like enchanted ground.
> One thought Content the good to be enjoyed;
> This every little accident destroyed.
> The wiser madmen did for Virtue toil,
> A thorny, or at best a barren soil;
> In Pleasure some their glutton souls would steep,
> But found their line too short, the well too deep,
> And leaky vessels which no bliss could keep.
> Thus anxious thoughts in endless circles roll,
> Without a centre where to fix the soul.
> In this wild maze their vain endeavours end:
> How can the less the greater comprehend?
> Or finite Reason reach Infinity?
> For what could fathom God were more than He.

No one would claim the presence of powerful or complex poetic thought for these lines; nor of the speculating Hardy type of thought. Nor have the rhymed ideas the compelling personal quality of feeling that Yeats's thought has. But we feel them superior to the Wordsworth in their relying less on the validity of the explicitly stated idea's content, which is a matter for philosophy, than on the poet's management of and attitude towards his materials: Dryden is present as poet in a way that Wordsworth is not. For Wordsworth's ponderous and abstract blank verse, we have an easy and rigorous handling of the couplet. And the skilfully used couplet has an air of finality about it which the more solemnly-intentioned blank verse misses: the rhymes seem to clinch the matter in hand and at the same time, adding to the easy-going and near-conversation manner, ensure that the matter is not heavily laboured. The sustained play of the poet's lightly-mocking and amused attitude over his material imparts to it a unity beyond that which it possesses

by virtue of logical progression of thought; the latter sort of
unity would be present if the ideas were expressed in prose,
but the former is the poet's only. The satiric poet in Dryden
gives life and attractive expression to what is after all only
second-hand material. His disbelief and mild contempt of the
old philosophers, who 'blindly groped' and 'rashly judged'
(the sounds of the contrasting phrases help to suggest their
satirical tone), are shown to be well grounded when he
laughs at the conclusions they reached: for he can quickly
and easily prove their failure to find an absolute truth and
recipe for mankind. He skilfully belittles them with good-
natured laughter. The line about 'every little accident', set
against the previous solider and deliberate one, suggests by
the way it slips along how easily the 'Content' school of
philosophers were nonplussed. The irony of the paradoxical
'wiser madmen' is followed up with a metaphor which,
though common enough, does suggest the positive obstacles
and unproductive labours that appertain to the life of
strict 'Virtue'; but what gives that line its particular flavour
is the conversational 'at best', where we hear the poet's
voice slightly raised in a phrase which is the more telling
for being seemingly off-hand; seemingly, but it will be
noticed that its 'be' emphasizes 'barren' – a good example
of alliteration functioning unobtrusively. 'Glutton' is the
more forcefully scornful for its having a physical application
normally; the full phrase 'glutton souls' is strong by its
sound and by the way it unites the physical and vulgar
'glutton' with the bodiless and pure soul. There is truth as
well as laughter in the picture of the Pleasure devotees fail-
ing to find an ultimate satisfaction; they are felt to be unquestionably dismissed in the rhythm which stresses their
shortcomings, especially in the middle one of the three lines,
where nearly every word receives an assumed-solemn
emphasis: 'But found their line too short, the well too deep';
'leaky vessels' by sound and by conception ridicules the
pretensions of the seekers; the whole metaphor, throughout
the three lines, is of the kind that deflates the seriousness and
dignity of the subject. The poet's skill in mockery succeeds
in making us feel the absurdity of the efforts to find a fixed

point for these thoughts which 'in endless circles roll', and his last line has an admirably and justifiably final ring about it. These lines of Dryden are offered here as a demonstration of a way in which argument can be successfully incorporated into poetry. It is poetry that we are enjoying, not the argumentation as such. The material in itself doesn't matter much to us until the poet has made it come alive. It is the poet's voice that matters.

To conclude the section on a strongly positive note, indicating two different ways of functioning of poetic thought, different but having certain fundamental elements in common, we can consider first a poem by Blake, then an excerpt from *Antony and Cleopatra*. Here is Blake's 'A Poison Tree':

> *I was angry with my friend:*
> *I told my wrath, my wrath did end.*
> *I was angry with my foe:*
> *I told it not, my wrath did grow.*
>
> *And I water'd it in fears,*
> *Night and morning with my tears;*
> *And I sunnèd it with smiles,*
> *And with soft deceitful wiles.*
>
> *And it grew both day and night,*
> *Till it bore an apple bright,*
> *And my foe beheld it shine,*
> *And he knew that it was mine,*
>
> *And into my garden stole*
> *When the night had veil'd the pole:*
> *In the morning glad I see*
> *My foe outstretch'd beneath the tree.*

The prose-meaning of the poem, the prose-thought, could be extracted to run something like this: 'As soon as I told my friend that I was angry with him, the anger died away; but when I was angry with my foe, I cherished the anger, and by cunning and deceitful behaviour I laid a trap for him which was his undoing.' This is what a simple summary would be like; and the extent of its inadequacy, despite its significance as a psychological 'truth', to suggest the range and depth of experience that the poem covers, is some evidence of the presence of extraordinary poetic thought. Blake is concerned to express certain psychological facts: the release from an emotion or an attitude – anger here – that takes place when such an emotion or attitude is given utterance and comes into the open; the change from anger, when it is hidden, into the evil of dissimulation; the 'sweetness' and evil of revenge. But the facts are given a strange and complex potency, quite beyond what their value as 'true' facts can give, by the manner of their presentment. The manner is that of a vision described with great clarity and definiteness. The poet is giving clear and vivid utterance to most subtle and ambiguous feelings; and it is the union of clearness of vision and complete simplicity of language with the profound ambiguity of his attitude that gives the poem its power. The poet is both good and evil: he is good and wise to speak openly to his friend, he is evil to use his wisdom, which degenerates into cunning, to overcome his foe. He is clear-headed and deliberate, but there is perhaps a touch of remorse, though no relenting, in his 'fears'; and his 'tears' are real as well as assumed. The 'smiles' and the 'soft deceitful wiles', noted down as evil, are at the same time felt to be delightful, and the sinister apple is a beautiful thing. The ambiguity continues to the end where the poet is 'glad' at the murderous victory he has won. A further ambiguity is felt in our recognition of the 'honest' confession of dishonest behaviour. Nearly all the poem is concerned with the development of the metaphor out of the word 'grow'; after the first verse of six short statements, and springing spontaneously out of it like natural growth, there is a marvellously easy and sure transition to the vividly concrete setting and action, out of which we can *extract* the prose-meaning, but *in* and *through* which we feel the wealth of the poet's *experience*, experience understood and controlled with such certainty as to be felt inevitably and profoundly true. Consider the way in which the statements and the narrative work. In a poem of sixteen lines there are some sixteen clauses (not one to each line however), and nearly every line is in a sense self-contained, yet so perfectly does the action 'grow' out of the initial terse but easily natural 'logic' that the poem is a most forcefully coherent whole. There is no feeling of thoughts having been clothed picturesquely; the vision, which is one of action, moves directly, the thought is fused in it. And it moves, not just by its intrinsic quality as vision, but by the inevitability and suggestiveness imparted by the poet's language: vision and language are one. The repetition of 'And' gives deliberateness and relentlessness, and this impression is enhanced by the quiet, even movement maintained throughout, the climax coming with the greater force for its being calm. But though the movement is quiet, it is emphatic; the speech-rhythm is heightened in such a way as to stress unostentatiously the key words, and analysis would show the rhymes to be magnificently used: it is unnecessary to demonstrate here a point that is so clear, but we may briefly note how the stresses in the first verse fall in the main on 'angry', 'friend', 'told', 'end', 'angry', 'foe', 'not', 'grow'; the verse movement and the sound work with this kind of unforced emphasis throughout. The pattern of the poem is regular, but its regularity is functional; that is to say, the pattern makes for the clarity, the certainty, the coherence, of the poetic statement. It seems the only possible expression for the ordering of the experience that led to the poetry. Through the low tones of the beginning of the stratagem and the insinuating sibilant sounds associated with his smiles and soft deceits, the temptation to gloat is felt to be growing, but it is never allowed to get out of hand; and after the shining apple has been seen by the foe (who is also an intending deceiver), the stealth of his action is suggested in the quiet falling quality of the words that describe it. The climax gains its great force by its being the culmination of an evil and inevitable-seeming process, by its quiet certainty, and by the juxtaposition of 'glad' with the 'foe outstretch'd beneath the tree', where the poet's acceptance, uneager but assured, shocks despite his having led us with such certainty to such a culmination. The horror of his exultation is the greater for its being controlled. The word 'outstretch'd' contributes powerfully: it is a 'physical' word, its sound, even its appearance, emphasizing its meaning; and not only is it the more impressive for appearing against the glad and gladdening morning ('glad' can go with both 'morning' and 'I'), where, this being the time of the sun's rising and of birds' singing and of other manifestations of brightening life, its presence suggests more horror and 'ambiguity'; but it is also in strong meaning- and sound-contrast with 'stole': 'stole' ... 'outstretch'd' – the stealthy act, the retribution; the word may also suggest 'outdone'. Comprehensive analysis of the poem would reveal further implications: the significance of the conjunction and opposition of day and night, for example, and the mystery of darkness; the suggestion of Satan in the Garden of Eden, and the apple of the tree of knowledge. The poem provides a superb example of poetic thought: the experience of the duplicity of human behaviour is given concrete embodiment – the apple shines there for all of us – in the simple-complex action centring round the Poison Tree. It is a visionary, not a mystical poem; for though at some points we may not be sure of the precise prose-meaning (for instance, has 'veil'd the pole' a significance beyond its mysterious suggestiveness? is the pole or pole-star emblematic of guide, conscience?), fundamentally we feel the profound 'meaning' of the vision, which is not oddly personal but has a universal human application. And we feel it not because of Blake's penetrating psychological faculty – though that is of course here in the poem – but because of his power to express his experience in words that are strong and vivid.

In *Antony and Cleopatra*, after Antony has been excitedly and over-buoyantly giving voice to his determination and hopes about the coming fight against Octavius, Enobarbus says:

> *Now he'll outstare the lightning. To be furious*
> *Is to be frighted out of fear; and in that mood*
> *The dove will peck the estridge; and I see still,*
> *A diminution in our captain's brain*
> *Restores his heart: when valour preys on reason,*
> *It eats the sword it fights with.*

The plea for reason, the dispassionate comment on its necessity in human conduct, is not made in general terms but is linked naturally to, fused with, comment on a particular man in a particular situation, and is expressed with sharp vividness. The maxims 'To be furious Is to be frighted out of fear', and 'when valour preys on reason It eats the sword it fights with', are given an added impressiveness by their being part of this wise and balanced speech; the quiet, steady movement of phrases 'and in that mood' and 'and I see still', balanced evenly with each other, help to give a sober certainty of tone which is itself an admirable comment on Antony's furious valour. Enobarbus makes five main points, progressing from the first half-caustic but controlled remark about Antony to the final vividly metaphorical generalization; and the basis of the poetic thought of the passage, holding and binding these points together, is Shakespeare's conception of the folly of courage without reason. A feeling of something which seems violently anti-natural and yet is a part of nature inspires the lines. Antony is felt as a man who is somewhat grotesquely challenging nature and defying destiny: the eyes with which he confronts Jove's lightnings are wild and staring; he is a mortal foolishly pitting himself against a natural force. 'Furious' suggests his attitude, and Enobarbus's paradox, emphasized by the alliteration, is entirely and wisely true: the furious man doesn't fear, but his fury is itself the outcome of his being afraid to face circumstances with a considering mind. This generalization is given substantial and vivid support by the image of the dove pecking the ostrich: this is a fact of nature, but like Antony's staring it is felt to be ludicrously ineffectual and verging on the monstrous, the more especially as the dove is a symbol of gentleness and peace. There is, however, some modification of this sense of abnormality in nature: Enobarbus condemns Antony, but there is no touch of personal scorn or dislike in his attitude; and though Antony is belittled by the introduction of the pecking dove, he, like it, has 'heart'; and when the whole speech is taken in, 'Now he'll outstare the lightning' is felt to contain admiration as well as blame. However, calm analysis, and cool, regretful

censure of the 'diminution of our captain's brain', remains
the predominant note. The absurdity of over-emotional,
self-deceiving behaviour, culminating in disaster, is superbly
expressed in the final statement. When we read 'preys on'
we recall the 'foolish' dove pecking at the ostrich, attempting the impossible; then by a sudden, swift change of direction which nevertheless continues and intensifies the meaning, the poet presents Antony 'furiously' destroying himself
(Antony is called a 'sworder' elsewhere in the play). The
last image, the climax of the rapid but controlled flow of
instances of 'unnaturalness', shocks with its concreteness –
'eats the sword': the hard, sharp steel in the throat – and
yet is inevitably right here because it is at one with the
'truth' of the thought that has already been established;
and the movement and emphasis of 'It eats the sword it
fights with' almost exactly echoes that of 'The dove will
peck the estridge', so that this human judgement seems as
right as the natural fact is true. The last clause has also a
kind of definite sharpness and clarity of sound which drives
home the monstrous nature of such a suicide. The certainty
of tone of the speaker, the poise that comes from his
balancing of dove against estridge, brain against heart,
valour against reason, and from the corresponding balancing, already commented upon, of certain rhythmical units –
all the balancing occurring effortlessly as a natural part of
the supple speech-rhythm of the whole – are a strong factor
in the full effect of the poetic thought. The main source of
the power of the passage is in the union of concepts and
instances of violent or grotesque behaviour and phenomena
with the tone of quiet and assured good sense. And the
'quiet' good sense is that of wide experience; the images are
those of a man of observation, knowledge, travel, action;
Enobarbus is not a theorizer. There is a dry deliberateness
of intonation and movement which carries the spirit of a
disenchanted man of action. And the disenchantment is not
of that debilitating kind that degenerates into lethargic
cynicism; it goes with a lively and varied play of mind.
The speech fuses idea, description, illustration, argument,
images; and it is mostly in terms of things seen and felt,

senses and feelings engaged. Its unity (note how it begins and ends with an image of bright swiftness connected with danger) is of that developing kind given by an extraordinarily flexible imagination moving easily and swiftly from one image or illustration to another as it plays consistently upon its theme.

This concluding paragraph may usefully recapitulate some main points. The subtlest and most significant thoughts of philosopher, psychologist, anthropologist, etc. do not become poetic by virtue of their mere inclusion in poetry: the poetic thinker is the poet. Sometimes the poet falls to versifying philosophy, etc. for no valid poetic reason; and some poets (there are parallel cases in prose, of course) owe much or most of their fame to this. But the poet as such uses language which more than conveys his thought; it enforces it by its movement, its sound, its imagery, it gives it vividness and often an underlying wealth of meaning; the language is the sure evidence of his particular and individual grasp of the 'thought'. To alter his language would mean altering and impairing his thought; whereas in expository and informative writing (which, let us remember, forms the great bulk of all writing), the language might be altered considerably and still convey the same meaning. 'Meaning' in this sense is only a part of the poet's expressiveness; his experience is not a matter of gathering ideas and facts at second-hand; it is one of sensuous, emotional, and intellectual awareness of life. His thought, in his poetry, is felt through the way his words work. Ideas existing in the abstract and for their own sake do of course interest him and have significance for him, but if they are incorporated into his writing they find embodiment in expression that comes home to mind and senses and feelings with strength, clarity, precision, vivid immediacy. It will be obvious by now that rhythm, sound, imagery, diction, feeling, are inseparably bound up with discussion on poetic thought; and the further we proceed with our examination of the various 'elements', the more we shall come to realize the organic quality, fusing all elements, of the finest writing.

Chapter 5

FEELING

The quality of our living, as human beings, depends very largely on the kind and quality of our feelings, and the quality of our feelings depends partly on our having learned to distinguish true from false feeling, and on our readiness to accept for ourselves, when necessary, the readjustment consequent upon such a recognition. The aim of this section will be to examine some of the implications of 'true' and 'false' and to show how some feelings are 'better' and more valuable for our living than others.

It would be widely agreed, in a general way, that a person with a wide range of feelings has a fuller life than a person with a more restricted range; and that we are alive when we are feeling freshly, or profoundly, or delicately; and that lack of all feeling is death or unconsciousness. But certain distinctions we can make within the scope of these propositions are by no means widely recognized; for instance, that fresh, strong feeling in an individual person is a different thing from the mass strong feeling in the people at a football match or a dog track, or at a political meeting; or that some types and manifestations of feeling are gross self-indulgence and are not at all the thing they appear to be; or that an appearance of strong feeling may be only a mask hiding some weakness or other.

Again, in this connexion most people would agree as to what is good and what is bad – in a general way: depth and strength of feeling are good, superficiality, shallowness, and absence of feeling are bad; control is good, lack of control is bad; in a crisis the calm man is more useful than the hysterical man; and so on. But it is not always easy – it certainly doesn't come 'naturally', it has to be learned in one way or another – to know our own feelings, to say nothing of other people's; it is not always easy to say confidently, 'This is desirable and that isn't; this is useful, that is useless'. Control of powerful feeling, for example, may look like lack of feeling, to an insensitive observer; and conversely, mere vehemence may be mistaken for strength.

Our growing-up involves the rejection of some feelings and the development of others: for instance, we learn to 'place' the enthusiasms and fads of childhood and early youth, as we get older. We don't read the same books with the same emotional attitude towards them as we did when younger, nor pursue the same hobbies. We have to learn to curb, in some situations, displays of disappointment, grief, exultation, etc.; we try to prevent the display of our emotions from being an embarrassment to other people. But while most of us outgrow the feelings belonging specifically to 'childish things', not all attain a full maturity, which implies having some understanding of our feelings, and having control over them or management of them when necessary.

An extremely valuable thing that literature can do for us is to reveal the existence of a kind of common basis of feeling; that is to say, in literature we come in contact with expression of feeling in a way that is rarely possible in actual life (because so much feeling is hidden or disguised for one cause or another) and come to realize that others have had the same feelings as ourselves and have been able to understand them, bring them to light. It is a help to know that whatever difficult and intractable stuff we find in our own emotions, the same has been felt by others, and has been more or less satisfactorily understood by them, and so is no longer the source of a vague sense of frustration. This frustration-feeling is very prevalent; we often have vague feelings of dissatisfaction, cynical indifference and so on, and often we have no knowledge of their causes and so no possible means of dissolving them.

To learn to perceive, in writing, the reality and worth of the emotion in and behind it, is to help our emotional and intellectual growth. Such growth is not the same thing as mental precocity. Many young people who see 'adult' films and who seem to be so 'modern' and knowing in the ways of the world, are in reality emotionally backward. The kind of precocity that manifests itself in glib smartness in the grown-up manner is often a mask put on to impress others and at the same time to hide an inner feeling of uncertainty and weakness from oneself. Simply to say this is not to condemn that attitude: probably we have all done that sort of thing at some period of our lives. The reading of good writing will help mere precocity to develop into real growth.

Many 'grown-ups' remain more or less in the adolescent stage, emotionally. Never having learned to exercise any sort of detached judgement, they maintain naïve enthusiasms and antagonisms; in politics, for instance, they have a 'black-and-white' attitude, one side is all right and the other is all wrong; they support with unqualified fervour and assail with unqualified bitterness. Nor are such people ever aware that the position they have taken up with such simplicity may ultimately do their cause harm, or that their fervour and their bitterness may in reality be due to factors that have nothing to do with politics; they may be allowing, perhaps unconsciously, some sense of personal failure to affect and colour excessively their views and their relations with other people.

Again: those members of an audience who unthinkingly and sentimentally identify themselves with the hero and heroine of the film they are watching, are doing the same thing as a boy does when he unconsciously becomes the School Captain or the record-breaking aviator of the book he is reading at the moment. They are indulging in adolescent day-dreaming and self-dramatization. In youth, this sort of indulgence is quite natural and in many ways valuable. But prolonged and carried on right through 'adult' life, as judging from the nature of the most popular books and plays and films it is to an alarming degree, it is surely to be deplored; because, being an easy surrender to romance as an escape from and as compensation for the difficulties of actual life, it prevents the growth of the emotional and intellectual qualities which could deal satisfactorily with those difficulties. Ultimately, 'romance' of the popular kind fails to satisfy; like a drug, it is something taken over and over again with a sort of desperation, to fill up a gap.

Much popular so-called serious entertainment has elements of sham love, sham heroism, sham grief, sham religious fervour. The purveyors of these emotions and attitudes, whether on film, radio, stage, in the printed word, are really displaying a kind of vanity, exhibiting their 'personality' with a show of emotion. It is common even in good drama to see and hear actors giving over-emotional displays, putting themselves before the play and so distorting it. And unfortunately they get a lot of applause. There is no need to over-act in a good play.

Many people seem to be easily deceived by a show of feeling. And many are too often at the mercy of their feelings, too easily ready to indulge them, to give vent to feelings which their judgement, if they allowed it to operate, would make them question the value of. An audience may enjoy the idealistic insincerities of a song like 'Trees'; the singer no doubt sings with 'feeling', the audience responds with 'feeling'. But there is a sense in which the feelings, though apparently strong, are 'false', for it is certain that the people who are so easily carried away and exalted by the tune-cum-words, not allowing themselves really to grasp the words (and there is both ignorance about robins' nests, and incongruousness in the image of nesting in the 'hair'), are deceiving themselves about their feelings with regard to trees. We should probably be right in saying (speaking generally) that they are by no means the most likely kind of people to observe and appreciate, to 'feel', the real living tree. It would be good to hear the comment of a genuine tree-knower and tree-lover like Cobbett, on an effusion like 'Trees'. The trouble is that such sentimentality in 'art' has the effect of diminishing or impairing the development of real feeling. Further: people who are such an easy prey to their own worked-up feelings are also easy prey to anyone who wishes to turn those feelings to his own advantage. It seems to become easier and easier for ambitious statesmen to induce, by 'clever' emotional appeals disseminated by all the latest contrivances, that form of mass-hysteria which is so useful to them in some political and economic situations. Mass-feeling is easily twisted this way and that by unscrupulous power-seekers.

A proneness to sentimentality, then, can have bad practical issues. By 'sentimentality' we mean, briefly, feelings that are too easily let loose, and which will be found on consideration to be more a weak indulgence than deep authentic expression. And sentimentality manifests itself in many ways. 'Toughness' in writing, for instance, is often a mask for an inner emptiness. Much hearty and manly-seeming writing is as sentimental, because forced and worked-up, as a tearful Victorian song.

It is interesting, too, to note how ready people are to laugh at the sentimentality (of the obvious kind) of other ages while being apparently unaware of that of their own. We smile at the cheap emotion in this verse from a Victorian song:

> *O hear the sweet voice of the child!*
> *That the night winds repeat as they roam!*
> *O, who can resist that most plaintive of prayers? –*
> *O father, dear father, come home!*

Yet many people who would rightly smile at this absorb uncritically many of our present-day popular songs whose words are equally fatuous and whose tunes are often suggested by those of the Victorian age.

The examination of the passages that follow will be in the main concerned with the endeavour to show that true emotion and what we may here call emotionalism find very different modes of expression. Many writers, indulging in emotional orgies themselves, seek consciously or unconsciously to give their readers the same sort of 'enjoyment'; they flatter their readers that the possession of feelings of whatever kind is in itself a good thing, and they account it laudable to be able to 'move' their readers. Yet it is an extremely simple matter to do this; it can be done with a few stock emotive words. To give a most obvious example: rhyme 'June' with 'moon' and 'love' with 'stars above' and you have the basis of a poem or song which with banal, cheap, and worthless feeling will find a response in large numbers of people. We must be on our guard against becoming complacent when we speak of maturity, which in its fullness is so difficult to achieve; but we aren't necessarily being superior when we say that the people who make a habit of indulging in easy, undisciplined responses are immature in a very obvious way: there is no substance in their feelings. Good writers have strength, depth, delicacy, of feeling; bad writers make a show of possessing feelings, they are showy, superficial, crude, naïve, but sometimes they are clever in covering up their deficiencies. We have done a great deal for ourselves when we have learned to discriminate between the sensitive in feeling and the insensitive. For falseness of feeling, in writing as in life, manifests itself in many ways, some of them very cunning; the 'June ... moon' sort of writing, with its stale, second-hand, general (that is, not individual) quality of feeling, is perhaps the simplest and commonest exemplification of all.

The idea that poetry is *par excellence* an outpouring of emotion that has little or nothing to do with intellect is still common. I once heard someone say that Goethe, 'like Shakespeare', was 'a singing bird'. The description is romantically simple; for the naturalness, the seeming spontaneity, of Shakespeare and of other great writers, is not a 'thoughtless' flow but is something that rises out of a wonderful union of feeling and judgement. Nor is it any evidence of an emotion's lack of strength that it is under control; the emotion may be extremely powerful and yet be controlled; control is not the same as suppression, as shutting out the feelings, which is, obviously, bad. A man at the mercy of his feelings is immature. And a writer with 'strong' feelings but without control of them is an immature writer. When Dickens gave his feelings a loose rein, the effect on his writing was harmful and sometimes disastrous; for instance, when he was unable to control his resentful feelings about America and to see them in their right proportion, he produced in *Martin Chuzzlewit* those descriptions of the valley of Eden which are quite unconvincing because they are grossly exaggerated: distortion – and in this case truth and not caricature was Dickens's aim – is the result of his

lack of control over his feelings. He was not, in this instance, sufficiently an artist.

When a good writer is expressing feeling he does it with the greatest possible precision. We shall see that this does not entail hair-splitting analysis on scientific lines, nor anything in the nature of lengthy exposition of inessentials. Rather it is a matter of finding exact and telling expression for an attitude which is the result of having felt the implications of a situation as fully, as inclusively, as possible. One man, watching a liner depart, may have a wider range of subtle and complex feelings and a greater knowledge of them, than another man watching the same ship. As readers we both intensify and clarify our feelings when in contact with the worth-while writer; the way in which he has approached and ordered his experience helps us, by deepening and widening and refining our awareness, to order ours. If he holds beliefs strongly he does so as a result of having thought long and deeply about life: he has no crude 'one-way' feelings and attitudes. He tries to harmonize conflicting feelings in himself; for instance, he may be what we call 'progressively' inclined in politics and yet dislike the mechanization of the land, and in this situation there is no ready-made solution at hand to harmonize these contradictions; integration can only come, if at all, from honest and precise 'exploring' of his feelings and thoughts. Human life has perhaps never been 'simple' to live; and in our time, with the process of 'dehumanization' (a temporary phenomenon perhaps) due to excessive regard for the machine and to the machine-mind and its mania for classification and management from the outside, and with so much knowledge and so many theories on so many subjects, it tends to get more difficult and complicated. We need to know our minds and feelings in the middle of all the diverse claims and voices of life. The good writer can help us in ways very different from those of the advocators of cure-all policies and of the purveyors of comforting doctrines. In situations where feelings are involved, which means virtually all the situations that we meet in life, he has both living feeling and a knowledge of his feelings. Instead of the vague, loose, and often muddled and often conventional feeling-expression of the inferior writer, he gives something individually and sharply felt.

The passages that follow are examined for the kind and quality of feeling that they contain. Broadly speaking, it is the distinction between true and false feeling, between real and unreal, that is the object of our investigation. That 'broadly speaking' is necessary because the subject is a very extensive and complex one, and we can do no more in the space at our disposal than touch it at a few essential points.

One of Shelley's most celebrated love-lyrics is 'The Indian Serenade':

> I arise from dreams of thee
> In the first sweet sleep of night,
> When the winds are breathing low,
> And the stars are shining bright:
> I arise from dreams of thee,
> And a spirit in my feet
> Hath led me – who knows how!
> To thy chamber window, Sweet!
>
> The wandering airs they faint
> On the dark, the silent stream –
> And the Champak odours fail
> Like sweet thoughts in a dream;
> The nightingale's complaint,
> It dies upon her heart; –
> As I must on thine,
> O! beloved as thou art!
>
> Oh lift me from the grass!
> I die! I faint! I fail!
> Let thy love in kisses rain
> On my lips and eyelids pale.
> My cheek is cold and white, alas!
> My heart beats loud and fast; –
> Oh! press it to thine own again,
> Where it will break at last.

The popularity of this poem for a certain type of reader, and perhaps for most readers at one stage or another, is easily accounted for: the poet invites participation in what we feel bound to call an indulgence of emotion, making use of a simple rhythm to purvey his 'romantic' wares. That is perhaps not the fairest way of putting it; it isn't intended to suggest that Shelley is consciously exploiting the responses of his readers in the manner of those writers (and advertisers) who seek only popularity and profit. The poem is offered by the poet in perfectly good faith. But though it has its own kind of 'sincerity', we feel, because of the absence of any particularly realized situation that could possibly justify such an outburst of emotion, that a romantic situation has been created almost as an excuse for the outpouring. The poet provides the general and popular elements of romance: dreams, sweet sleep, winds 'breathing low', bright stars, and so on. And because of the potent emotive quality of these elements, many readers fail to perceive that the poet is only vaguely gathering them up together and inducing vague emotion in both himself and themselves. 'Champak' is a definite epithet but it serves no real purpose; it doesn't make the experience more definite or vivid for us (and the poem is for us though it is an *Indian* Serenade) because we haven't experienced those 'odours', and are told nothing about them; the word is introduced for suggestiveness of the glamorous-exotic kind. The poet is staking everything on emotional effect: 'sweet', one of the most popular words in the language for evoking a vague sentimental response, occurs three times; 'Oh' also occurs three times; there are ten exclamation marks. No reason is given or hinted at for the turning of the joyful expectations into weakness and despair. There is little justification for the misuse of 'faint', 'fail', and 'dies' in the second verse; the fact that there is a certain consistency of feeling behind them doesn't excuse their 'untruth' in their context; they are merely emotive words here, serving to enhance the pervading swoon-desire feeling. The poet is rather thoughtlessly attributing his own attitudes and feelings to the airs, the odours, and the bird's 'complaint'. And when the words come again in the last verse they are in an unimpressive order. The whole poem has an air of unreality in spite of – or perhaps because of – the poet's violent assertions of his feelings and of his bodily presence; 'impalpable' phrases like 'a spirit in my feet' and 'like sweet thoughts in a dream' add to this impression of unreality. On the credit side of the poem may be put a simple verbal music of the alliterative-assonantal kind. And it could also be said that the poet does achieve his object: that his rather breathless rhythm does convey his feelings. This is certainly true, and it is the main point that we make against the poem. For the perfunctory movement carries only a kind of excitement; and apart from their headlong quality, the feelings are not what they claim to be. For far from the poet's really thinking of death, he is, we feel, indulging in an emotionalism which gives him and many of his readers considerable satisfaction. We must of course be on our guard against becoming too easily superior about this kind of poetry: a spokesman for 'romanticism' might argue that expression in the manner of 'The Indian Serenade' is more life-enhancing than otherwise, and that such effusiveness is at least better than a tight suppression of feeling. But though we would not wish to identify ourselves in such a matter with the attitude of the hard-boiled man of the world, we should probably agree that such a surrender to emotionalism is a comparative weakness and would not be made by a more disciplined poet.

Thomas Hardy, in one of his earliest poems, presents a situation in a manner quite different from Shelley's; and though the situation is by no means similar to that in 'The Indian Serenade', a comparison between the two poems is interesting because Hardy's situation could easily, in lesser hands, have given rise to the kind of feeling and expression of self-pity which is part of the emotionalism accompanying Shelley's. The poem is finely entitled 'Neutral Tones':

> We stood by a pond that winter day,
> And the sun was white, as though chidden of God,
> And a few leaves lay on the starving sod;
> – They had fallen from an ash, and were gray.
>
> Your eyes on me were as eyes that rove
> Over tedious riddles of years ago;
> And some words played between us to and fro
> On which lost the more by our love.

The smile on your mouth was the deadest thing
Alive enough to have strength to die;
And a grin of bitterness swept thereby
    Like an ominous bird a-wing. ...

Since then, keen lessons that love deceives,
And wrings with wrong, have shaped to me
Your face, and the God-curst sun, and a tree,
    And a pond edged with grayish leaves.

In its colour references, and more especially in its sound and
movement, the poem finely suggests the appropriateness of
its title; and emotionally, too, it has a kind of impressively
'neutral' quality. That is to say, it is not personal in the
sense of making vehement affirmations about the poet's
condition. It *is* personal, however, in that there is presented
an individual, precise experience; and by the manner of
presentation its emotional undertone is powerfully conveyed. The utter tonelessness of several of the lines – 'They
had fallen from an ash, and were gray': the sound is as flat
as it well might be – and the drab and niggardly natural
background contain and suggest the feeling of disillusionment. But the dissillusionment is not that of the adolescent
disappointed in love; the mind and senses are awake: in that
last-quoted line he names the tree, he marks the colour of
the once-green leaves. The seeming apathy of nature and
the indifference of the woman of the past are the 'inspiration' of the poem; Hardy is far from apathetic himself,
though the poem is in a sense so bleak. Reserves of strong
emotion are felt through phrases like the sharp and hard
'chidden of God' and 'starving sod'; 'wrings with wrong'
has a similar strength; 'God-curst sun' is strongly felt, the
definite and terse sound of the challenging phrase standing
out in the otherwise quiet line and giving to the coolly-
said 'your face' and to 'and a tree' some of its own emotional
force. The past situation, in the poet's exact memory, is
analysed coolly; he now knows it for what it was, sees her as
keeping up some sort of an appearance and himself as join-
ing in with 'meaningless' words. The paradox in the third
verse emphasizes vividly both her shallowness and the
strange lifelessness of which the poet is so sharply aware. It

is especially bitter to him that the only real vitality she evinced was in the 'grin of bitterness' which 'swept' her mouth. What might at first reading seem a forced comparison between a 'grin' and an 'ominous bird' is found to be apt; the last verse gives full evidence that her behaviour was an indication of what he might have expected in the future; the simile is one of those that strike with a quality of unlikeness as well as of likeness. 'Grin' has a sardonic force; and the realization now of what her eyes then signified is bitter to the poet, but the bitterness is not petulant, or spiteful, or impotently revengeful, and is contained with poise in the dispassionate analysis: 'some words played between us to and fro' works strongly by understatement, and quietly reduces the past situation to the significance it is now seen to have had. The calm, seeming-matter-of-fact but actually bitterly felt first line of the last verse – the movement is sure and deliberate, the assonance of 'keen' and 'deceives' is functional and not just musical – is given additional strength by its juxtaposition with 'wrings with wrong': the apparently commonplace 'love deceives' is felt here as a personally experienced 'truth' not only because of the convincingness of what has led up to it, but also by its being coupled with the individual phrase 'wrings with wrong', which makes a kind of physical, immediate impact. Intensity of feeling, a controlled intensity, is felt through the calm of this last verse. And the return to the 'pond edged with grayish leaves' brings home the winter barrenness of the landscape, in which, we remember, the sun was 'white'. Hardy's landscape without warmth is an integral part of the total experience of the poem. The emotion of this poem is not affirmed in the first person; disillusionment is not here an occasion for crying emotional wares. If we compare the tone of

> *Since then, keen lessons that love deceives,*
> *And wrings with wrong, have shaped to me*
> *Your face ...*

with

> *Oh lift me from the grass!*
> *I die! I faint! I fail!*

we feel that Hardy is mature in the way he can stand apart from and evaluate his experience; he can 'distance' his subject, while Shelley is immersed and half lost in his. Emotion is under control; there is depth, not turbulence; he is restrained where Shelley is demonstrative; his experience is ordered where Shelley's is chaotic. By the way in which the disenchanting experience is faced and calmly though movingly assessed, we are made aware of the poet's strength. (It may be stated here that this comparison of two particular poems is not intended to represent a comparison between the complete *œuvre* of each poet.)

Our next poem should be immediately recognized as an example of false feeling. It is not a poem of the overcharged variety; it is something less defensible than that. It is a palpable example of 'poetical' manufacture, where a trivial fancy is exalted into an affirmation of idealistic feeling. When false feeling is the accompaniment or the result of the self-deceptiveness of immaturity, we ought to be more concerned with pointing out, and enlightening where we can and as well as we are able, than with censuring. But there is little excuse for a writer's being so lacking in honest self-criticism as to let pass a poem like the following; it is called 'Sunday up the River', and it is by the nineteenth-century James Thomson (it finds a place in the *Oxford Book of English Verse*):

> My love o'er the water bends dreaming;
> It glideth and glideth away:
> She sees there her own beauty, gleaming
> Through shadow and ripple and spray.
>
> O tell her, thou murmuring river,
> As past her your light wavelets roll,
> How steadfast that image for ever
> Shines pure in pure depths of my soul.

The worthlessness of the feeling here will be immediately apparent to most readers; we want to be as sure as we can that we know why we recognize it as worthless. The evidence that the poet's protestation is merely a protestation uninformed with genuine feeling, is plentiful and pervasive. To begin with, the rhythm is trite throughout: no fresh, individual feeling would find expression in such a mechanical, frivolous lilt. It is similar in its slickness to that of the Victorian song previously quoted – 'O father, dear father, come home!' The poet imposed the smooth monotony of a ready-made rhythm on to his content, imposed it 'from outside'; that is, the rhythm was chosen as a 'poetical' one and the content was easily manipulated to fit it. Nothing receives emphasis in this movement which is quite divorced from the accent and inflexions of the spoken language; no variety of movement conveys any 'shift' or nuance of feeling. The whole sound of the poem tells us that the poet skimmed over his subject, as it were, and conventionalized it in the most 'poetical' fashion. Then there are the hackneyed verbal 'poeticalities': 'o'er', 'glideth' (repeated), 'thou' (followed by 'your', incidentally), 'wavelets'; and a spate of clichés: 'my love', 'beauty gleaming', 'murmuring river', 'steadfast', 'shines pure', are some of them. Such a collection of verbal clichés of the sentimental-idealistic kind makes it plain that the experience behind and expressed in the poem is both commonplace and vaguely apprehended; this is the more deplorable in a poem of such professed exaltation of feeling. The flimsy basis of the poem – the fancy of a comparison between the two images – will hardly stand examination: 'shines' in the last line is inappropriate when applied to the 'depths' where her image is said to be, and is there mainly for its 'easy' emotive appeal when associated with 'pure'. The repetition of 'pure' is distastefully self-righteous.

Browning's 'Meeting at Night' is in theme near enough to Thomson's poem to provide an illuminating comparison:

> *The gray sea and the long black land;*
> *And the yellow half-moon large and low;*
> *And the startled little waves that leap*
> *In fiery ringlets from their sleep,*
> *As I gain the cove with pushing prow,*
> *And quench its speed in the slushy sand.*

Then a mile of warm sea-scented beach;
Three fields to cross till a farm appears;
A tap at the pane, the quick sharp scratch
And blue spurt of a lighted match,
And a voice less loud, thro' its joys and fears,
Than the two hearts beating each to each!

It doesn't require a second reading to feel the immense
superiority of this to 'Sunday up the River'. We have to
ask, Where does the superiority lie? In what ways is this
poem better than that? Our first impulse is, probably, to
point to the elements in the poem which convey the strong
sense of actuality; and certainly it is good to be in contact
with a real journey and to be made sharply aware of the
'tap at the pane' and of the match being lit; these 'fiery
ringlets' are a world away from Thomson's 'light wavelets'.
It is good to be brought close to a setting which is not falsi-
fied by idealization; the 'slushy sand' is as much a part of it
as the 'yellow half-moon'. Browning imbues the scene and
situation with genuinely exciting character, making it vivid
as he succeeds in conveying his feelings of expectation, excitement, happy fulfilment. This success is a poet's success;
that is to say, it is by his management of words, and not by
virtue of the data of the 'realism' referred to above, that he
creates experience in a poem. There is no vague gesture
here towards any kind of self-magnifying attitude, but an
experience keenly felt and accurately described in all its
interesting particularity. The first two lines, slow and suggestive in sound in a manner reminiscent of Tennyson but
less formal, more 'real' in their speaking-voice rhythm, are
an admirable foil for the lively movement describing the
waves; but more than onomatopoeia is involved. The stages
of the journey are presented in such a way as to convey the
lover's feelings as well as and simultaneously with his
physical activities. After the long row, making apparently
slow progress on the 'gray sea' ('apparently' because of the
wide immensity of the background), the scene is brought
vividly close as he comes near the shore, and at the same
time, with accurately descriptive words like 'startled',
'leap', 'fiery', the poet suggests something of his tense and

eager feeling; the *scene* is apprehended and expressed
vividly because his *feelings* are quick and alert. The last two
lines of the first verse with their words of strong physical
and sensuous properties – 'gain', 'pushing', 'quench',
'slushy sand' – and their forceful movement passing into
thick and clogged inactivity, enact the conclusion of the sea
journey. The quickness of 'Then a mile' suggests the poet's
haste, which is then slightly and aptly modified by the full
and enjoyed 'warm sea-scented beach'. The three fields are
swiftly crossed, suitably given the briefest and simplest attention; and the swift efficiency of the lines leading to the
culmination is sufficiently in evidence – the vitality coming
from the sharp concreteness of the words and the alert,
quick movement – not to need detailed comment here. The
last two lines are given in exactly the same way as the other
eight or ten 'items' which have been expressed with such
decisive clarity, and by virtue of their position they derive
added emotional force from the preceding hastes and eager-
nesses and anticipations. They are a true emotional climax;
the exclamation mark is not of that kind that tries to inject
into words an emotional significance that they don't really
hold. So Browning conveys his feelings, not by telling us how
fine or strong or deep or everlasting they are, but by the
vivid and vigorous presentation of a situation through
which the feelings emerge; and, of course, the feelings are
worth conveying: the poet's aliveness is in the alive language. The poem is not offered here as a great love poem; by
the side of Donne's 'Nocturnall', for instance, or Marvell's
'The Definition of Love', with their amazing union of
powerful with subtle and complex feeling, it would appear
limited. Its scope is not large, emotionally or intellectually.
But within its limits it has vividness, energy, and intensity.
A complete analysis would reveal more sources of its impressiveness.

   Browning is not always, perhaps not even often, as impressive as this in achieving the expression of emotions or
attitudes which are significant for him. The following lines
come from what the poet himself probably intended to be,
and what is generally accepted to be, a more 'important'

poem than 'Meeting at Night'; they are from 'Abt Vogler', the poem of the organist who is praising God:

> *Therefore to whom turn I but to Thee, the ineffable Name?*
>   *Builder and maker, Thou, of houses not made with hands!*
> *What, have fear of change from Thee who art ever the same?*
>   *Doubt that Thy power can fill the heart that Thy power expands?*
> *There shall never be one lost good! What was, shall live as before;*
>   *The evil is null, is nought, is silence implying sound;*
> *What was good, shall be good, with, for evil, so much good more;*
>   *On the earth the broken arcs; in the heaven, a perfect round.*
> *All we have willed or hoped or dreamed of good, shall exist. ...*

This is an affirmation of faith. But without suggesting that the poet is being hypocritical – he most obviously isn't – we can say that the affirmation has a somewhat hollow ring about it. Is it not too loud? is not the self-assurance akin to the blustering vehemence of a man who reinforces his arguments with thumps and a ringing voice? And this kind of self-confidence is of course more apparent than real. Browning is asserting the inevitable triumph of good, and this in itself isn't objectionable, however inclined to debate it we may feel (his manner seems to challenge debate). But what is unacceptable to many readers is the peremptory and cocksure tone – 'What, have fear of change ...' and 'The evil is null, is nought ...' – in which evil is played down. His attitude is here the naïve black-and-white one: the imperfections of earth against the perfection of Heaven; and in his attempt to impose it on his readers he becomes dogmatic and strained. (A most valuable comparison could be made between Browning's approach and that of T. S. Eliot; in 'The Four Quartets' the 'problem of evil' is the subject of the most scrupulous, searching, and profound exploration.) Instead of the quiet or steady tone of certainty that goes with real belief, there is a feeling of strain; the exclamation marks, the capital letters, the ejaculation 'What', the overdone 'shall', taken together are evidence that there is more self-persuasion than inner conviction in the poet's belief (we are entitled to say 'the *poet's* belief' because Browning clearly intends us to endorse the words of his musician). We don't quarrel with the passage because

it is optimistic but because we feel that the optimism is
forced: there are too many dogmatic statements; mature
experience doesn't speak with such a buoyant voice in such
general terms about good and evil. The passage is too hearty
and expansive; the rollicking rhythm reveals the insensitiveness of the feeling behind the words. And though the
passage (it is characteristic of the whole poem, which has the
same tone throughout) certainly evinces a vigour in the
handling of the language, we feel that it is a rather factitious
vigour, the words and manner being too imposing, and that
Browning's talent (or genius) is here operating in regions of
experience for which his feelings were not sufficiently
subtle, sure, and true.

One of Hopkins's simpler poems, 'Pied Beauty', is in all
essential respects a contrast to Browning's ministerings:

> Glory be to God for dappled things –
>   For skies of couple-colour as a brinded cow;
>   For rose-moles all in stipple upon trout that swim;
> Fresh-firecoal chestnut-falls; finches' wings;
>   Landscape plotted and pieced – fold, fallow and plough;
>   And all trades, their gear and tackle and trim.
> All things counter, original, spare, strange:
>   Whatever is fickle, freckled (who knows how?)
>   With swift, slow; sweet, sour; adazzle, dim;
> He fathers-forth whose beauty is past change:
>   Praise him.

Where Browning tries almost to bludgeon us into accepting
his asseverations, Hopkins seems to let his poem speak for
itself; there is no zealous desire to convert in his 'Praise
him', And it isn't necessary to share Hopkins's actual religious beliefs before we can feel the reality that religion is
to him; for he provides concrete evidence of at least one of
the bases of his beliefs: and that is, his love of the sensuous
world. So that his God is very much more than a 'Builder
and maker ... of houses not made with hands'. The first four
words of the poem, in themselves a commonplace, are immediately shown to be no conventional piety when they
come up against the unexpected and homely 'for dappled
things'. The 'Glory' isn't a general unrealized quality which

is part of a vague gesture of homage; it is given a rich substance in the keenly observed and enjoyed items of 'pied beauty'. The poem is not one of Hopkins's most powerful poems; it is a poem of 'simple-true' feeling rather than of powerful feelings. This feeling is conveyed through his delight in the things he has observed and which he presents in surprising and accurate, concrete words. But though the feeling may be called a simple one of love and praise, the choice of the 'dappled things' indicates a far wider range of interests than is manifested in the 'Abt Vogler' poem; the various items, united by the quality they have in common, have an extremely varied range of attitudes and feelings associated with them: skies, cow, coloured trout, chestnut leaves and fruit, the land, the tackle of 'all trades', 'fickle, freckled' things. But despite this variety, indicating a range of awareness lacking in Browning's 'one note' poem, the feeling-attitude of the poem remains simple. A comparison of the last line but one with Browning's 'What, have fear of change from Thee who art ever the same?' shows the fundamental difference in tone; where Browning offers a rather blustering confidence in God's constancy, Hopkins quietly states the 'truth' that an unchanging principle maintains the very variety and 'piedness' of the changing sensuous world. And the restraint of the last line is one of steady thankfulness, without smugness – the objects he lists have often a homely beauty, he is never solemn – and is at the opposite pole to Browning's asking God for better things, for that is what we feel he is really doing in attempting to talk evil away. (A complete analysis of this poem would deal especially with the quality of the words, their texture, their sound, and with the way they are placed and ordered. It would be shown how the poet's particular 'sensibility' reveals itself in a certain sharp and close vividness of language.)

Any feeling that is made to appear more important than it really is can be called inflated. In its simpler manifestations (for it sometimes assumes cunning forms) it is fairly readily recognized, and yet, as we have already hinted, in 'practical life' even the everlastingly familiar 'noble gesture'

– arm flung forward, ringing voice, etc. – is fatally impressive for large numbers of people especially when they are in a crowd. Many people will laugh at and condemn, in their individual judgements and when they are alone or in a small group, the moral and emotional pretentiousness whose effect, when they are in a crowd, they succumb to. And in writing as in oratory, it is easy to make an impression on the uncritical. Sometimes the inflation isn't of the obvious 'shouting-out' kind. The cinema and hosts of modern best-selling novels provide heroes of the 'strong, silent' type, men of action and not of words, and whose noble intentions shine in their steadfast eyes and decisive mouths and chins; the well-groomed type with a light in the eyes is still very much with us. He should be quietly deflated by the critical reader and spectator, wherever he is met with.

The instances of false feeling that we have so far examined in this section have all been in one way and another 'inflated'. This paragraph will briefly refer to that kind of feeling which is so obviously pretentious that it ought immediately to be recognized and 'placed'. There is a celebrated passage (it is in the *Oxford Book of English Prose*) from Scott's *The Talisman*, describing how King Richard of England behaved when faced with an antagonistic Austrian crowd. The whole passage, which it is not necessary to quote in full here, has the fault of inflation to such a degree that the incident which is meant to be overwhelming in effect, fails to impress us as anything but quite unreal. Richard bursts his way through the crowd 'like a goodly ship under full sail, which cleaves her forcible passage through the rolling billows, and heeds not that they unite after her passage and roar upon her stern'. This sort of exaggeration is intended to make us feel Richard's power; it fails to impress because it turns the episode into something superhumanly 'heroic'. The simile pictures an ideally victorious and triumphant thing, and does it in a romantically popular manner; and with its adjectives that help to evoke a 'stock response' – 'goodly' ship, 'full' sail, 'forcible' passage, 'rolling' billows – and its 'poetical' cadences, it assumes an interest of its own in its (conventional) sugges-

tion of power, and so detracts from the actuality of Richard's
passage through the crowd. The scene hasn't been imagined
or grasped in its particularity; it has a basis of action of only
the general and vaguely-realized kind. Richard goes on to
speak 'in a tone which seemed to challenge heaven and
earth'. Richard's gestures and actions are no less magni-
fied than his voice; everything is heightened into super-
human proportions. The author seems here to have lifted
himself into a state of forced exalted feeling; in his admiration for the 'heroic' he allows his writing to become pomp-
ous and insensitive.

Yet the man who wrote of King Richard in such a strain
was also the author of 'Proud Maisie':

> *Proud Maisie is in the wood,*
>   *Walking so early;*
> *Sweet Robin sits on the bush,*
>   *Singing so rarely.*
>
> *'Tell me, thou bonny bird,*
>   *When shall I marry me?'*
> *— 'When six braw gentlemen*
>   *Kirkward shall carry ye.'*
>
> *'Who makes the bridal bed,*
>   *Birdie, say truly?'*
> *— 'The grey-headed sexton*
>   *That delves the grave duly.*
>
> *'The glow-worm o'er grave and stone*
>   *Shall light thee steady;*
> *The owl from the steeple sing*
>   *Welcome, proud lady!'*

The feeling in this poem is the reverse of inflated; it can't
be pin-pricked, for it doesn't make an exhibition of itself.
In fact, one wonders whether 'feeling' is altogether the right
word to use in connexion with a poem like this, though a
substitute doesn't easily suggest itself. Certainly the poem
hasn't the kind of personal feeling that informs, in different
ways, 'Neutral Tones' and 'Meeting at Night'. But beneath
the scene and the dialogue, which comprehend the 'meaning' of the poem, is something that we feel impelled to call
deep feeling. It is not personal emotion; it is the feeling that

accompanies the 'steady' realization of the fact of death; it seems in fact to reside in the realization as expressed with the poet's peculiar force. It is objectified, so that the circumstances of the poem seem to be universally applicable and not to refer to the 'proud lady' only. The situation is presented in a detached manner, and being without any affectation of sentiment or language the whole poem has an impersonal note which makes it inevitable-seeming. The underlying feeling is one of solemnity, but it is a solemnity which goes with humour of the 'grim' but lively kind. The colloquial ease and simplicity of the language, with 'Sweet Robin' – could there be a pleasanter preacher? – making his two-edged replies in this equivocal marriage-funeral situation, carry an immeasurably more serious feeling than all that language about ships and billows and earthquakes. And the 'six braw gentlemen' are *there* in a way that Richard and his foes are not: the humorously serious feeling in this reference to the coffin-bearers is felt in the very sound of the sure and starkly accurate adjectives. The reminder of old age comes unobtrusively in 'grey-headed sexton'; and 'grave' has additional emphasis by its alliterative and assonantal association with 'grey'. The robin's answers stand sure and 'grim' against the pert and tripping 'Tell me, thou bonny bird' and 'Birdie, say truly'; but in spite of this, and although the poem ends (almost) with graveyard, steeple, and owl, the tone never becomes edifyingly moralistic. The rhythm is kept easily flexible, with a conversational emphasis on the key words; note for example how surely the movement and sound of the last verse suggests the 'steady' nature of the glow-worm's light and the still hardness of 'grave' and 'stone', and how finely the sense is carried over from the last but one to the last line, both 'sing' and 'Welcome' receiving ironical emphasis. This 'sing Welcome', in association with the steeple and the owl, is the culmination of the pervasive mingling of the solemn and the mocking; in itself it is a positive note, as is the robin itself 'singing so rarely' on the bush, and the glow-worm's light, and the vigorous activity of the sexton. There is a beautifully maintained balance of feeling throughout, between these living elements and the warning of mortality. And we feel that it is right that the 'proud lady' should be still alive at the end, after being admonished. Scott's attitudes, then, towards his respective subjects in these two pieces are in strong contrast with each other. In this he is ironical, detached without being formal, genuinely and 'humanly' serious; in that he was uncritical and unwisely enthusiastic. This economical vernacular poetry carries a strength of controlled feeling; it was false feeling that found expression in that bombastic prose.

Inflated writing, the effect of unduly elevated feeling in the author, is not to be confused with the expression of intensity of emotion. And intensity of emotion is itself a very complex subject and needs keen discrimination in discussion. Romeo feels intensely, and so does Antony (in *Antony and Cleopatra*); we attribute 'passion' to each of them. We ought to be able to perceive from their speeches – by the evidence of the language, and not only by explicit comment provided by Shakespeare – that Romeo's is the vehement, 'blind' passion of immaturity, while Antony's, despite its fallibility as a 'guide to life', is that of a man of maturely passionate feeling.

Here is the characteristic Romeo speaking; Friar Laurence has just told him that for killing Tybalt he has been sentenced not to death but only to banishment:

> *Ha, banishment! be merciful, say 'death';*
> *For exile hath more terror in his look,*
> *Much more than death: do not say 'banishment'.*

And when the Friar points out that he is after all only being banished from Verona and that he is being treated mercifully, Romeo continues:

> *There is no world without Verona walls,*
> *But purgatory, torture, hell itself.*
> *Hence-banished is banish'd from the world,*
> *And world's exile is death: – then 'banished'*
> *Is death mis-term'd: calling death 'banished',*
> *Thou cutt'st my head off with a golden axe,*
> *And smilest upon the stroke that murders me. ...*

'Tis torture, and not mercy; heaven is here,
Where Juliet lives; and every cat, and dog,
And little mouse, every unworthy thing,
Live here in heaven, and may look on her;
But Romeo may not: — more validity,
More honourable state, moure courtship lives
In carrion-flies than Romeo: they may seize
On the white wonder of dear Juliet's hand,
And steal immortal blessing from her lips. ...

This may flies do, when I from this must fly. ...

The feverish excitement is felt in the movement which pours on and on (in the play it continues in the same way for a considerable distance beyond this point) as the speaker submerges himself in the one subject – his deprivation – that engrosses him. And the high-pitched tone combines with the hyperbole of the content-items to produce a kind of naïve obsessiveness which can be called 'blind'. Romeo has no control over his feeling. Unable to control his feeling to the 'pattern of events' (which it would actually be greatly to his advantage to do), he is wrapped up in himself; for him there really is 'no world without Verona walls'. This emotionalism is a verbose thing, too. Despite his 'grief', Romeo enlarges with considerable deftness on the theme of banishment, ending up this first passage with the pretty metaphor about the golden axe. He exaggerates: 'be merciful, say "death"', 'terror in his look', etc.; he makes the utmost of his complaints: 'purgatory, torture, hell itself', 'and every cat, and dog, And little mouse, every unworthy thing'. The crowning example of the distortion produced by his emotionalism is where he attributes 'more validity, More honourable estate, more courtship' to the 'carrion-flies', turning them into editions of himself. He dramatizes himself in the third person. His weak pun in the last line is obviously 'worked'. And yet, despite all the effusiveness, there is a certain intensity; not an intensity of grief, as Romeo claims it to be (grief doesn't make claims for itself), but an intensity of youthful passion, a passion we can call self-ignorant and self-displaying. Finally, while we feel the force of the flow of poetry, carrying with it a kind of simple

inverted ecstasy, and while we may sympathize with the
speaker's unhappiness, we feel also that Friar Laurence's
comment is just: 'What simpleness is this!'

Thyreus, a servant of Octavius, who is Antony's rival for
the Empire, has been offering Cleopatra terms from his
master, and at the moment of her giving him her hand to
kiss, Antony enters with Enobarbus. He speaks:

>   *Favours, by Jove that thunders!*
> *What are thou, fellow?*
>
> THYREUS: *One that but performs*
> *The bidding of the fullest man, and worthiest*
> *To have command obey'd.*
>
> ENOBARBUS [*aside*]:   *You will be whipt.*
>
> ANTONY: *Approach, there! – Ah, you kite! – Now, gods and devils!*
> *Authority melts from me: of late, when I cried 'Ho!'*
> *Like boys unto a muss, kings would start forth*
> *And cry 'Your will?' – Have you no ears?*
> *I am Antony yet.*
>
>   [*Enter* ATTENDANTS]
>   *Take hence this Jack, and whip him.*
>
> ENOBARBUS [*aside*]: *'Tis better playing with a lion's whelp*
> *Than with an old one dying.*

The feeling of Antony manifested here, however blame-
worthy it may appear by the standards of a Christian or a
prudent morality, has nothing of the raving note in it. The
extremity of anger, which is due not merely to Cleopatra's
offering favours to an inferior, but to a despair about his
waning fortunes (as Enobarbus shrewdly points out),
doesn't prevent his language from being clear, terse, and
definite; while the speech-rhythm is superbly varied to
carry the changes in the direction of the feeling. On entering, he immediately takes in the unexpected situation, and
his feeling about it is spontaneous and certain; his ejaculation is angry and suggestive in itself of jealousy, violence,
and punishment: 'Favours, by Jove that thunders!' 'Fellow'
is sharply contemptuous, as is the tone of the whole sentence
in which it appears. As soon as he learns who Thyreus is (he
has probably guessed it for himself by now), his peremptory
call to the attendants is as quick as his first perception and

speech were on entering. A moment's attention is given to Cleopatra; 'Ah, you kite!' is not vaguely abusive and savage, but has appropriate reference (in Antony's mind) to her as a person trafficking in garbage, as that bird does; she is also dark-tawny coloured. Impatience makes him violently break out with 'Now, gods and devils!' the seemingly insignificant 'Now' helping to emphasize the insistence on haste. But the angry impatience, far from blurring his mind, seems to give it a sharp edge. The slight delay of the attendants brings home to him afresh the realization of his position, and there is 'sober' truth and pathos in his description of it, making the surrounding angry expressions all the more compelling. 'Melts' suggests inevitable dissolution; and the simile 'Like boys unto a muss' (a muss is a scramble for money or prizes), and the juxtaposition of the colloquial 'muss' with 'kings', suggest his pride and scorn with economy and directness. The movement of these middle lines finely conveys the note of regretful but lively 'reminiscence' as he waits, commenting truly on himself. The sharpness returns with 'Have you no ears?' and the rather pathetic 'I am Antony yet' is both rebuke to the attendants and, as he probably half realizes, encouragement to himself. His final words – 'Jack' is a term of utter contempt; we may think too of jackdaw, cheap-jack, jack-in-office – are precise and sure in their monosyllabic simplicity; 'Take hence this Jack' is commandingly deliberate in movement, and 'whip him' is sharp and tight-lipped. Enobarbus's comment is just and fitting; anything like the Friar's 'Thou fond mad man' to Romeo would be irrelevant if applied to Antony. Enobarbus accepts the force of Antony's passion, seeing it for what it is: the inevitable accompaniment of the waning fortunes of a powerful man, and as such a phenomenon as natural as the dangerous mood of an old, dying lion. (We have dealt almost exclusively with Antony's feeling in this passage, stressing its reality as against the speciousness of Romeo's. An examination of the 'feeling' behind the whole situation as here presented would reveal a good deal more than we have spoken of: for instance, the total feeling is slightly but subtly modified by the [humorous] rapidity with which the forecast 'You will be whipt' is fulfilled. Enobarbus knows his Antony.)

'Maturity', as applied to human life, is one of those abstract words with profound and subtle implications. It seems impossible to define it shortly, and it is difficult to give any account of it that we could confidently call comprehensive. We should probably all agree that Antony is more mature in feeling than Romeo. But we should by no means be in agreement as to whether a 'completely mature' man would be subject to such a passion of anger as Antony's. However, we should probably postulate, as a condition of maturity, a full and harmonious emotional life ('harmony' needs discussion, too), and this would involve a considerable degree of understanding of one's emotions, the cultivation of some and the rejection or modification of others helping to determine our actions and behaviour. When we add to all this the capacity to enter imaginatively into other people's minds and feelings, and the ability to exercise a discriminating and evaluating judgement, and further, the ability to record such 'feeling' and 'judging' experience with vitality, precision, and power, then the main conditions for a great writer exist. It was because Shakespeare came to possess, in the course of his developing experience, such qualities in such a supreme degree, that he is our greatest poet.

Chapter 6

DICTION

ROBERT BURNS prefaced his poem 'Address to the Deil' with two lines from 'Paradise Lost'. His poem shows that he was prompted to do this by the humour that he found in the thought of the difference between Milton's and his own attitude towards sinning mankind. The two lines are these:

> *O Prince! O Chief of many throned Pow'rs,*
> *That led th' embattled Seraphin to war;*

and his own first verse runs:

> *O thou! whatever title suit thee,*
> *Auld Hornie, Satan, Nick, or Clootie,*
> *Wha in yon caverns grim an' sootie,*
> > *Clos'd under hatches,*
> *Spairges about the brunstane cootie,*
> > *To scaud poor wretches!*

(spairges: scatters; cootie: wooden kitchen dish.) What it is wished to emphasize here, however, is not so much the difference in attitudes as the contrast in diction (which is due to the different attitudes, of course): on the one hand the racy and colloquial Scots, on the other the 'Grand Style'. It is not intended to compare the two poets generally, nor to embark on the great modern debate on Milton's style and his place and influence in English poetry. But with what is implied in Burns's juxtaposition we may suitably put a remark or two made by Keats. Keats says in a letter that he decided to re-write 'Hyperion' because he came to realize that his verse was too self-consciously Miltonic, self-consciously 'artistic'; 'English ought to be kept up,' he writes. Again, there is no question here of comparing Keats and Milton. Keats's intention in 'Hyperion' was in any case different from Milton's in 'Paradise Lost', and Keats knew the uselessness of imitating, and the dangers of being unduly influenced by, another writer's style. The main purpose of this section will be to discuss some different classes of words and some different ways of using them, and in this discussion the *positive* implications of Keats's 'English ought to be kept up', will, it is hoped, be made clear.

'The hot sun made us sweat.' 'The high-temperatured rays emanating from the luminary of day caused us to perspire.' The first of these sentences isn't at all distinguished, but it needs no great critical insight to perceive that it is better than the second, and we can easily enough give the grounds for our preference. Simple and obvious as the example is, it can serve as an introduction to a consideration of two vital points concerning the use of language: one, that concrete and 'physical' words are likely to make a more forceful and immediate impact than general and abstract ones; two, that straightforwardness in language is more telling than round-about and superfluously elevated expression. This second point is subject to qualification in that 'straightforwardness' is not to be confused with simple ordinariness; and inversion of language is often a strong element in a writer's, especially a poet's, most 'natural' and 'straightforward' mode of expression. It is when inversion is *unnecessary* that it becomes a 'poetical' affectation. With reference to the first point: if we were as conscious of the significance of words as we might be, we should feel a certain physical force even in words like 'emanate' and 'perspire': both these words had originally some physical connotation (as can be seen from the dictionary). Nevertheless, our first sentence remains undeniably the more effective.

In an essay called 'The Noblest Monument of English Prose', J. L. Lowe states: 'Most of the words we use today to express intellectual, emotional, spiritual concepts had originally physical significance. "Wrong", for instance, originally implied something twisted; "implied" itself involves the idea of something folded within another thing – as "involve" rests on the concept of something rolled or wrapped about. "Concept" itself goes back to the notion of seizing or grasping; to "consider" was first to gaze attentively on the stars; "attentively" again rests ultimately on the idea of physical stretching. ... But with us these vivid physical implications of the words we use have all become attenuated, they have faded out. ...' It is certainly true that for the great majority of us the physical implications of most words like those quoted in this passage do not exist; not consciously, at any rate. The usage of language tends inevitably to become superficial and glib through its frequency. We use a word like 'powerful' without feeling that it is really 'power-full'. We do not seem today to taste the full flavour of words as we feel that Falstaff (and Shakespeare, and probably his audience) tasted them when he was applauding the virtues of 'good sherris-sack' which makes the brain 'apprehensive, quick, forgetive, full of nimble, fiery, and delectable shapes'. And being less aware of the life and substantiality of words, we are probably less aware also of the things and qualities that the words stand for. It doesn't seem quite true, however, to say that 'with us these vivid physical implications ... have faded out'. For being an essential part of a word, they can never be entirely lost – only covered over and obstructed. It is part of the work of good poetry and of prose to restore that concrete, tactile, physical sense, bringing back into the word not only more 'body' but also greater precision and greater suggestiveness. This can be done only by an artist who, experiencing exact states of feeling, a particular emotion, conveys them by a use of words that cuts through the fogginess normally overcovering, blurring, those words, and so restores to them some of their basic and original meaning. Generally speaking, Saxon-derived words are nearer to the first 'primitive' meaning and quality; the Latin-derived words have travelled farther from it, with prefixes and suffixes often tending to pale them into near-abstraction. But, obviously, there can be no question of outlawing any word in the language as unsuitable for poetic use; 'malleability', 'preposterous', 'annunciation', can be livingly used in poetry as well as 'horse', 'hard', 'sky'.

Mr Eliot, both by his teaching and by his example, has shown in our age that there is no specifically 'poetic' language, that there is no bar against the most unlikely-looking words. A deep study of 'Four Quartets' is of immense value for what the poet says about his struggle to master the use of words, and for the superb command of language displayed there. There is a high proportion of abstract words in this poetry; but they are always used with precision, with regard for their particular force and effect; they are incorporated in the strong rhythmical expressiveness, and often they are set off by the 'simpler' concrete words. The following passage from 'The Dry Salvages' is given to demonstrate the magnificently successful union and interaction of concrete with abstract words. The poet is contrasting (though to put it in this way doesn't adequately suggest the profound process that is present in the poetry) the kind of 'time' symbolized by the waves' action in ringing the warning fog-bell with the 'time' conception that dominates our modern consciousness, imposing a slavery of anxiety. A full analysis of the passage would have to deal with the integration of content with movement, of prose-meaning with emotional suggestiveness. Details of diction should be thoroughly examined: the fittingness and particular force of words like 'chronometers', 'calculating', should be noted – how their greater 'artificiality' is *used* to help to convey the ethos and the activities associated with the notion of man-made time, so that they have a poetic and not merely a statement value. With them should be compared words and phrases like 'rung by the unhurried Ground swell', and 'Clangs The bell': strong, concrete words for the more elemental, more physical processes. It will be almost impossible, of course, to consider the words in isolation, apart from the total ordering of the language, but in view of what is to follow in this section a scrutiny of the passage from this standpoint of diction would be extremely useful:

> ... *And under the oppression of the silent fog*
> *The tolling bell*
> *Measures time not our time, rung by the unhurried*
> *Ground swell, a time*
> *Older than the time of chronometers, older*
> *Than time counted by anxious worried women*
> *Lying awake, calculating the future,*

Trying to unweave, unwind, unravel
And piece together the past and the future,
Between midnight and dawn, when the past is all deception,
The future futureless, before the morning watch
When time stops and time is never ending;
And the ground swell, that is and was from the beginning,
Clangs
The bell.

Where Saxon words are as a rule better (not better because they are Saxon – philology as such has nothing to do
with the appreciation of literature, though some writers may
gain from its study – but for having the qualities they have)
is in their greater *immediacy*, in the directness of their impact.
Latin words have added wonderfully to our language; and
in writing of the expository, ratiocinative, informative kind
they express ideas for which a purely Saxon vocabulary
would be insufficient. But in what we call 'creative' writing
– drama, novel, poem, essay – where a fuller and more
complex response is demanded, there will almost always be
found a bedrock of Saxon words. (There are connexions
here with the origins and development of language in an
agricultural community, with physical work in touch with
the soil and with the seasons and with growing things; but
the subject is too big and comprehensive to be embarked
upon in this context.)

It is best to call a spade a spade, unless there are good
reasons for doing otherwise. To call it '... the implement
rectangular That turneth up the soil' is the result of trying
to give the object significance by the use of 'impressive' diction; the actual effect is to dissipate the reality of the object
in a cloud of words and to achieve only portentousness.
Circumlocution, or periphrasis, gives the *words* a spurious
importance; spurious because the words exist over a kind
of void, something in the manner of florid ornamentations
or a façade on a building with weak foundations. A thing
isn't made more valuable by giving it a showy mask;
neither the lily nor the old tree stump needs gilding. When
Tennyson refers to the village church and communion
service as

... where the kneeling hamlet drains
The chalice of the grapes of God ...

he is showing more concern for the surface attractiveness of
his words than for the reality of his theme; the flowery
language, employed to impart an (unnecessary) added
dignity to the scene, tends to destroy that scene by calling
our attention to its own prettiness.

Every age seems to develop its own brand of false poetic
diction; and it could be shown how the lesser writers frequently, and the more considerable ones occasionally, draw
on its resources. The resort to such a diction is vicious in
that it precludes the possibility of finding genuine, individual expression for genuine, individual experience. When
an eighteenth-century poet was writing about fish he was
likely to refer to 'The finny tribe that rove the crystal
stream'. The attitude to fish, and to words, contained here,
is the reverse of freshly perceptive; 'finny tribe', 'rove',
'crystal stream', are all general conceptions, and in combination tend towards a kind of commonplace elegant ideal-
ism. How lacking they are in individual definition – in
'reality' – can be felt if we put them by D. H. Lawrence's
'gold-and-greenish, lucent fish', when he describes how,
when a boy, he has

Unhooked his gorping, water-horny mouth,
And seen his horrow-tilted eye,
His red-gold, water-precious, mirror-flat bright eye,
And felt him beat in my hand, with his mucous, leaping life-throb.

Here, we are made to see and feel the fish, to perceive something of its aliveness and strangeness as perceived with
intensity in the recollection of the poet. The actual, vividly
experienced, finds expression in vivid words. In the eighteenth-century line quoted above, the poet's 'experience' of
fish is revealed by the 'poetical' terms to be vague and
without real substance. It is picturesque to write 'the berries
that emboss The bramble, black as jet', instead of saying
simply 'blackberries', but Cowper is here only word-
spinning, however much he may have enjoyed seeing the
blackberry bush.

The dangers of adhering too closely to a chosen, pre-conceived style may be seen from the great example of Milton himself. Dr Johnson, who admired Milton greatly for many things, wrote of 'Paradise Lost' that 'the want of human interest is always felt'. He was thinking in the main of the paucity of human characters in the action and of the tiny amount of human experience available to the poet in the story he chose for his subject. But it seems likely that the remark was prompted also by the nature of Milton's diction. In part to compensate for, and perhaps to help to make less prominent, the unavoidable thinness of 'human' subject matter, Milton employed his Grand Style. Now it would be quite mistaken to stigmatize the Grand Style as inevitably pretentious, and to make a rigid identification of the 'natural' in writing with the genuine. As has been said before in this book, sometimes what looks like an unnatural way of writing is found to be the writer's most forceful and most 'natural' way of expressing himself. In the opening books of 'Paradise Lost' there is powerful writing of the heightened 'sublime' style; this occurs where Milton has a theme and characters that engage his imagination. But when he is present in the poetry more as self-conscious moralist and preacher, the poetry loses much of its fine vigour. Passages like the following – it is from Book VII – are characteristic of parts of the later books of 'Paradise Lost':

> Great things, and full of wonder in our ears,
> Far differing from this World, thou hast revealed.
> Divine Interpreter! by favour sent
> Down from the Empyrean to forewarn
> Us timely of what might else have been our loss,
> Unknown, which human knowledge could not reach;
> For which to the infinitely Good we owe
> Immortal thanks, and his admonishment
> Receive with solemn purpose to observe
> Immutably his sovran will ...

and it continues with words like innumerable, ambient, interfused. Most moderately sensitive readers will probably find this language stilted and too obviously aiming at a solemn impressiveness. Even when we take into account the seriousness of Milton's preoccupation with his religious theme, the strongest impression we have here is that of the monotonous solemnity of the language. The pages of 'Paradise Lost' have a very large number of words like circumfused, insensate, immutable, obdurate, unquenchable, invincible, inaccessible, omnipotence, corporeal. Keats went so far as to say that 'Paradise Lost', though 'so fine in itself,' was 'a corruption of our language'. To whatever extent we agree or disagree with this, it is fair enough to say that in deliberately setting out to achieve a Grand Style Milton lost touch with the life and variety of the spoken language, and so was in danger of becoming heavily inert and abstract in those places where his subject did not 'take fire' from his imagination. As an accomplished scholar, he was no doubt more aware of the 'physical implications' of his polysyllables than we, his readers, are; but as poet he doesn't always make us feel the *particular* quality of his words. It could probably be demonstrated that the finest poetry of Milton occurs when he is least conscious of the influences of the ancient languages. An opportunity will be found later in this book for the appraisal of a passage different in intention and effect from that quoted above.

'A selection of language really used by men': Wordsworth was in part driven by the 'gaudy and inane phraseology' of certain eighteenth-century writers to formulate the famous theory of which the above words are, from the standpoint of diction, the gist. His protest was on behalf of a greater reality and simplicity, as against the stereotyped affected literariness and the elegantly exalted attitude which those writers substituted for genuine expression of genuine feeling. Another remark by Johnson, this time about Gray, comes to mind here: 'He is tall by walking on tip-toe'. (Johnson excepted the famous Elegy from this stricture.) Wordsworth's theory was excellent as a reminder and a callingback to a less strained manner of writing. As an absolute it is unacceptable, of course; there has been great 'urban' poetry, and great complex poetry. But as a refreshing and revivifying force, as a protest against 'gaudy and inane phraseology', it was extremely valuable. By adhering to the theory 'on principle', and when he wrote without the full authentic urge to write living poetry, Wordsworth, as is well known, was often simply banal:

> And he is lean and he is sick;
> His body, dwindled and awry,
> Rests upon ankles swoln and thick;
> His legs are thin and dry.

And in his later work – the sap of his poetic vitality having dried up while he was still in his thirties – he tended to depart from his theory and to adopt a compensatory high-flown diction. But when he is at his best he shows astonishingly what can be done with unassuming language. The following passage from 'The Excursion' (it was written early in Wordsworth's writing life) gives part of the story of Margaret and the ruined cottage, as told by the old Wanderer to the poet:

> ... I see around me here
> Things which you cannot see: we die, my Friend,
> Nor we alone, but that which each man loved
> And prized in his peculiar nook of earth
> Dies with him, or is changed; and very soon
> Even of the good is no memorial left. ...
>
> Beside yon spring I stood,
> And eyed its waters till we seemed to feel
> One sadness, they and I. For them a bond
> Of brotherhood is broken: time has been
> When, every day, the touch of human hand
> Dislodged the natural sleep that binds them up
> In mortal stillness; and they ministered
> To human comfort. Stooping down to drink,
> Upon the slimy foot-stone I espied
> The useless fragment of a wooden bowl,
> Green with the moss of years, and subject only
> To the soft handling of the elements:
> There let it lie – how foolish are such thoughts!
> Forgive them; – never – never did my steps
> Approach this door but she who dwelt within
> A daughter's welcome gave me, and I loved her
> As my own child. Oh, Sir! the good die first,

And they whose hearts are dry as summer dust
Burn to the socket. Many a passenger
Hath blessed poor Margaret for her gentle looks,
When she upheld the cool refreshment drawn
From that forsaken spring; and no one came
But he was welcome; no one went away
But that it seemed she loved him. She is dead,
The light extinguished of her lonely hut,
The hut itself abandoned to decay,
And she forgotten in the quiet grave. ...

It is not of course simply the presence of a great preponderance of everyday words that gives this excerpt its quality. Such a presence, by itself, does not confer value; when, for instance, such words are used to express an experience which is assumed by the poet to be more significant than it is, the result is banality or bathos, as is felt in the quatrain above quoted, where the metre and rhyme only serve to emphasize the inadequacy of the prompting experience. Whether simplicity of diction is a virtue depends on the significance of what is being said. It is a negative kind of virtue (but still a virtue) in ordinary social usage; the usefulness of the dozens of workaday statements we make daily would be impaired or nullified if we began expressing their content in affected language. But their unaffectedness is not of that kind that carries a force of emotion or thought; their kind of simplicity is not the simplicity of this, for example:

> *And why take ye thought for raiment? Consider the lilies of the field, how*
> *they grow; they toil not, neither do they spin:*
> *And yet I say unto you, That even Solomon in all his glory was not*
> *arrayed like one of these.*

In the 'Excursion' passage, the 'feeling' of the words, allied inseparably with the pervasive feeling and tone and movement of the whole, is about as far from the kind of appeal made by high-sounding polysyllabics as any impression of words can be. The subject here could easily have been bungled; the way to sentimentality and heavy moralizing was wide open. But the poet's control is perfectly sure; the easy conversational tone, carrying such profundities of meaning, is never allowed to become chatty. Nor does the seriousness degenerate into self-important solemnity. Complete analysis would show a superb command of movement and emphasis, with subtle variations corresponding with the beautifully balanced interchanges, without any feeling of formality, of the actual-sensuous with the reflective and meditative. The recognition of the inevitability of transsience, of the continuous and silently-dissolving work of time, the sense of the inter-connexion of man and nature, the profound feeling for humanity, are conveyed with quiet assurance. We are dealing here with the kind of poetry in which the *tone* is the sure guarantee of the fineness of the experience. Wordsworth is not in the main using the active, physical, sensuous properties of words to make a strong impact; his words seem to flow out of the mood and attitude of mingled gentle reminiscence and profound contemplation, the profundity being merged in the human feeling. This profundity is felt as simplicity, so assured and true is the feeling behind the words; behind a reference like '... The useless fragment of a wooden bowl ...' there is a weight of human thought and feeling. The simplicity of the individual words throughout – they are everybody's words – is at one with the total attitude, and so is an integral part of a piece of writing in which the pathos of Margaret's life is merged in a deep and wide human sympathy.

The poetry of Hopkins would provide an excellent basis for a study of the properties of words. Such a study would reveal, in the case of Hopkins himself, that the finely controlled complexity and the dramatic intensity which are present in his best poems, are achieved through the use of words that have strong sensuous and physical properties. They are mostly simple words too, words that have connexions with fundamental human activities, with movement, with sense-perceptions, with the living interests of people, of English people in particular. And in revitalizing these words, recalling to us their wealth of suggestion and content, Hopkins has revealed, as all great writers reveal, the potentialities of the 'common tongue'. His complexity and so-called oddity (and sometimes he is bizarre; sometimes the result doesn't justify fully the strangeness of the manner) are not due to the use of unusual words, but to the unusual ordering of words, an ordering that was essential for the full expression of his distinctive sensibility. The words that we think of as most characteristic of Hopkins are words like these: round, fresh, gear, heart, fire, thwart, brim, fleece, rears, through, sweeps, sour, crisp, lace, tread, heave, steep, world, pack, hurl, bloom, rush, warm. These words are old, English words; they have a sensuous strength or fittingness, they do not simply convey a 'prose-meaning'; each word is unique. What the word 'heave' means is largely contained in the word 'heave'. But Hopkins doesn't use these words that have strong sound-qualities or muscular suggestiveness for simply musical, onomatopoeic effects; but to express with the greatest possible fullness the strength and stress of his emotion and thought. It would be useful at this point to glance back at the short Hopkins passages in the 'Imagery' and 'Poetic Thought' sections, and at 'Pied Beauty'. An examination of a single phrase like 'soft sift In an hourglass', or 'latch or catch or key to keep Back beauty ...' would help to confirm these remarks on language. 'Fresh-firecoal chestnut-falls', one of the 'dappled things' that delighted the poet, illustrates Hopkins's faculty of expressing his highly individual, imaginative 'vision' in common words; the common words are given vivid life. You may think of the shining, pied brown-and-whitish 'conkers' burst out of their shells, lying under the trees in autumn, or of the dapple of red and yellow leaves glowing with a fire of their own as coal glows with its own fire, giving out warm colour; it seems certain that Hopkins, whose extraordinarily quick eye and mind grasped the various patterns of things seen and of things thought about, meant both. The words are old and strong words, used freshly. The feeling of solidity in Hopkins's words, combining with the controlled energy that is felt in the movement and emphasis, helps to give the best of his poetry an astonishing immediacy and concentration. (Incidentally: one of the 'poetic dictions' of our day derives from Hopkins. A number of middling poets, lacking the real poet's emotional and intellectual experience that prompts the growth of an individual technique, are imitating his 'style'. A great or competent poet can and does profit by contact with the resources of expression revealed by other poets. But imitation of the *manner* alone will result in that kind of poetry which has surface qualities glittering above an inner poverty.)

The style at the opposite extreme to the simple and concentrated is the circumlocutory-cum-stilted. The central defect of this kind of writing is that it involves a departure from 'reality'; the substantiality of the subject is lost in verbiage, formal manipulation of words taking the place of language that carries the 'shifts' and development of feeling and thought and the sharpness of sense-perceptions. There is not a great fullness and concentration of experience behind the poetry of Edward Thomas, but if we compare a representative piece of his with a representative piece of Cowper, we shall see that he gets much more out of his simple words than Cowper does out of his 'poetical' ones. Here is the eighteenth-century poet describing a snow scene, in 'The Task':

> *The verdure of the plain lies buried deep*
> *Beneath the dazzling deluge; and the bents,*
> *And coarser grass, upspearing o'er the rest,*
> *Of late unsightly and unseen, now shine*
> *Conspicuous, and, in bright apparel clad*
> *And fledg'd with icy feathers, nod superb.*
> *The cattle mourn in corners where the fence*
> *Screens them, and seem half petrified to sleep*
> *In unrecumbent sadness. There they wait*
> *Their wonted fodder; not like hung'ring man,*
> *Fretful if unsupplied; but silent, meek,*
> *And patient of the slow-pac'd swain's delay.*

He goes on to describe the woodman, who only stops

> *But now and then with pressure of his thumb*
> *T' adjust the fragrant charge of a short tube*
> *That fumes beneath his nose ...*

and 'the feather'd tribes domestic'.

And here is a poem by Thomas:

> *Women he liked, did shovel-bearded Bob,*
> *Old Farmer Hayward of the Heath, but he*
> *Loved horses. He himself was like a cob,*
> *And leather-coloured. Also he loved a tree.*
>
> *For the life in them he loved most living things,*
> *But a tree chiefly. All along the lane*
> *He planted elms where now the stormcock sings*
> *That travellers hear from the slow-climbing train.*
>
> *Till then the track had never had a name*
> *For all its thicket and the nightingales*
> *That should have earned it. No one was to blame.*
> *To name a thing beloved man sometimes fails.*
>
> *Many years since, Bob Hayward died, and now*
> *None passes there because the mist and the rain*
> *Out of the elms have turned the lane to slough*
> *And gloom, the name alone survives, Bob's Lane.*

A concern to establish the all-round superiority of the Thomas passage would deal with the greater sense of reality that it gives, a presence of personal feeling that is lacking in Cowper, apart from his rather vague melancholy pleasure in the scene. It would be unjust to say that Cowper was not a 'true country-lover'; he has obviously seen the landscape he describes here, and has enjoyed seeing it. But though the visual details are evidence of personal observation, there is a lack of keenness in the language, and of an individual tone, that suggest a corresponding lack of keen perceptiveness in the experience. The impulse to write about the scene was not strong enough to make Cowper's writing compelling; in his desire to be and to prove himself a poet, he has used 'fine' language, and though the original experience is still discernible – in the noting of the details of the tall grasses, for example – it has lost, in being made into an artificial and 'literary' piece of writing, whatever 'edge' it may have had. The circumlocutory phrases – 'the verdure of the plain', 'the dazzling deluge', 'in bright apparel clad', 'half petrified to sleep In unrecumbent sadness', 'T'adjust ... nose', 'feather'd tribes domestic' – generalize and so to a degree falsify the experience. The piece isn't offensively bombastic; the worst we can perhaps say of it in connexion with feeling – apart from the all-over loss of sharpness discussed above – is that the attitude towards the animals is sentimental: 'mourn', 'sadness', 'meek', belong more to Cowper than to cows. We are dealing with a rather naïve verbal inflation in which what Cowper takes to be Milton's manner is incongruously applied to domesticated nature-cum-moral material. The placing of the (general) word 'conspicuous' is a simple example of Miltonic technique applied 'from the outside'; 'nod superb' and 'in bright apparel clad', which Cowper applies to grasses, might have been successfully used by Milton in a description of Satan and his host. In contrast, Thomas is quite unostentatious; no concern for verbal impressiveness interferes with his feelings of love and regret. The unforced humour of the first sentence, depending on our coming quietly at the end of it upon 'Loved horses', so qualifying the 'Women he liked' of the beginning; the emphasis, similarly unforced, given to certain 'living things'; the 'thought' of man's work, of the continuity of nature, of life and death, all find expression in a diction which is an organic part of the complete effect of a natural, feeling, speaking voice. The Englishness of the words is at one with the whole conception of and feeling about the English scene. And while not possessing the profundity of Wordsworth at his best, nor the rich and complex concentration of Hopkins at his best, Thomas's poem has its own individual accent. His words have roots in rural living; it is the everyday words, combining with the friendly tone and attitude, that help to bring 'shovel-bearded Bob' and 'Bob's Lane' near to us, whereas Cowper's words overlaid his scene and weakened its impact. Thomas's feeling has nothing to do with the conventional-romantic regret associated with the disappearance of the supposed idyllic. It doesn't exclude 'unpoetical' elements; and so, therefore, neither does his diction; he can quite naturally and without incongruity bring together the 'stormcock' (characteristically and suggestively using a local name for the misselthrush, that sings finely, and often in midwinter bad weather) and the 'train', and the 'nightingale' and the homely 'earned'.

'The effect of a natural, feeling, speaking voice': this phrase needs qualification. There would be such an 'effect' in the speech of neighbours arguing or chatting, and it is not this kind that our phrase has reference to. By 'natural, feeling, speaking voice', we mean a language indicating in its words and movement the worth and genuineness of the feeling beneath; it will not be swollen or stilted, and there will be no straining after mere metrical effects. The words and rhythms of the spoken language are arranged and controlled – it is an arrangement imposed by a controlled strength of feeling, not a mentally calculated one – with such subtlety as to appear like perfect spontaneous utterance; and in a sense it is spontaneous. A good piece of writing, springing perhaps out of prolonged emotion- and thought-experiences, often appears to be, from the impression we have of its inevitable 'rightness', as spontaneous as a growing thing. The Edward Thomas poem is unassuming and 'natural'; yet analysis would show its movement and emphasis to be subtly controlled to convey shades of feeling and development of theme, to indicate the degree of importance – the poet doesn't aim higher than his feelings prompt – that he attaches to his feelings and thoughts. Subtlety can exist with 'spontaneity', for which another name might be 'inevitability'.

Now there is another kind of spontaneity that is naïve and not subtle. Poetry with this sort of unaffectedness has little or no depth or pressure of feeling beneath it, little or no *control* of words for significant ends. Browning was a poet who realized that flowery phrase-making had to be challenged by the reintroduction into poetry of the vigorous potentialities of everyday speech. But, despite his frequent 'obscurity', there are places where he seems to have plunged into his work with a rather effusive simplicity, and we have the effect of something like a torrent of words, without much depth or direction. Here is a passage from 'Fra Lippo Lippi' where the gay artist-monk is telling the night-watchmen who have apprehended him, what sort of a childhood he

had and how he was introduced into the Carmelite mon-
astery:

> *I was a baby when my mother died*
> *And father died and left me in the street.*
> *I starved there, God knows how, a year or two*
> *On fig skins, melon-parings, rinds and shucks,*
> *Refuse and rubbish. One fine frosty day,*
> *My stomach being empty as your hat,*
> *The wind doubled me up and down I went.*
> *Old Aunt Lapaccia trussed me with one hand,*
> *(Its fellow was a stinger as I knew)*
> *And so along the wall, over the bridge,*
> *By the straight cut to the convent. Six words, there,*
> *While I stood munching my first bread that month:*
> *'So, boy, you're minded,' quoth the good fat father*
> *Wiping his own mouth, 'twas refection time, –*
> *'To quit this very miserable world?*
> *Will you renounce'* ... *The mouthful of bread? thought I;*
> *By no means! Brief, they made a monk of me* ...

No doubt this writing was spontaneous in the sense that the
poet wrote rapidly and easily. And no one is likely to deny
that it has its own vigour and a refreshing freedom from
stiffness. But why is it that, on a second reading if not at
first, it will be found not to satisfy as some of the other 'real
language' passages of this section satisfy? It is because we
soon become aware, in the absence of an illuminating subtlety of control of the words – control for the fullest effect –
of the comparative crudeness of the experience that the
words express. The passage illustrates that poetry can be
lively and amusing with very simple rhythms and everyday
words; but it shows also that the use of the words and
rhythms of the spoken language is not in itself a guarantee
of excellence. Browning's adaptation of such rhythms to
poetic use tends towards slickness; in spite of the skill with
which he varies his pauses, we feel a certain facility of movement which indicates that there is little 'pressure' behind
the words. Having little more than the emphasis of ordinary
chat, the resources of the words are felt to be easily ex-
hausted; there is not enough weight, no reserves of meaning

in its fullest sense, in them. We feel again how dangerously easy it is to write mediocre blank verse. The liveliness and vigour are there, in the intimate, chatty phrasing – 'God knows how', 'the wind' (not the wind that blows), 'Old Aunt Lapaccia', 'its fellow was a stinger', 'munching my first bread that month'; in the sarcastic touches – 'empty as your hat', 'the good fat father Wiping his own mouth'; in the irony – 'Will you renounce ...'; in the rapid movement. But the vigour is of the rather insensitive kind; it approximates to heartiness. Hence the sense of exaggeration and a brittle, seeming-certainty of tone that the passage gives. It could be argued that the manner of the writing is appropriate to the character of the speaker. But the value of the writing isn't enhanced by that consideration, in this instance; it is poetry we are dealing with, and not study of Fra Lippo's character, which is in any case so simple as presented by the poet that it requires no study. There is little variety in the poem, which is of considerable length; page follows page of the same kind of writing, and we feel in the end that the poet has become the slave of his own 'poetic diction'. And when Browning uses the same 'style' in his long argumentative poems, the chatty facility is often felt to be only an amusing skimming over the surface of his subjects, and strange and unexpected turns of fancy fail to be a substitute for deep involvement and searching exploration. But he was at least aware of the problem of the use of a live language as against the prevalent Victorian poeticizing that went with the uncritical, and therefore unprofitable, worship of the 'Romantic' poets; and at its best his language has an energy and a refreshing robustness springing from corresponding qualities of feeling.

Our last full example in this section is by way of a characteristic seventeenth-century poem. The poem is Herbert's 'The Collar'; the homely title has deep implications; with its simultaneous suggestions of rebellion against restriction and of the necessity of control, which is what it principally denotes, there is a secondary or complementary suggestion of 'choler':

I struck the board, and cry'd, No more,
                              I will abroad.
What? shall I ever sigh and pine?
My lines and life are free; free as the road,
     Loose as the wind, as large as store.
                    Shall I be still in suit?
     Have I no harvest but a thorn
     To let me blood, and not restore
What I have lost with cordial fruit?
                         Sure there was wine
Before my sighs did dry it; there was corn
Before my tears did drown it.
Is the year only lost to me?
Have I no bays to crown it?
No flowers? no garlands gay? all blasted?
                    All wasted?

Not so, my heart; but there is fruit,
     And thou hast hands.
Recover all thy sigh-blown age
On double pleasures; leave thy cold dispute
Of what is fit, and not; forsake thy cage,
     Thy rope of sands,
Which petty thoughts have made, and made to thee
     Good cable, to enforce and draw,
              And be thy law,
While thou didst wink and wouldst not see.
              Away! take heed;
              I will abroad.
Call in thy death's-head there, tie up thy fears.
              He that forbears
     To suit and serve his need
              Deserves his load.
But as I rav'd and grew more fierce and wild
     At every word,
Methought I heard one calling, 'Child';
     And I reply'd, 'My Lord'.

The poet is here simultaneously analysing the conflict in himself and presenting it in terms of human actions and gestures, of the senses and the body; and because the rhythm is strong and dramatically varied, the conflict comes home to us with vividness, with *immediacy*; we feel that it is being *enacted* for us in the words. The poem could be very profitably studied as illustrating what Mr Eliot has called attention to when he says that in much good poetry, especially that of the Elizabethan period and the seventeenth century, 'the intellect is immediately at the tips of the senses'. But our concern at this point is predominantly with the diction, and in this connexion we find that we have in this poem 'a selection of language used by men', in the sense that Wordsworth intended. Both imagery and diction are drawn from common human life, the imagery having a homely vividness and the words themselves a concrete strength. Things that can be felt and handled, smelled, tasted, fed on, things that affect the body, that prick it, that cheer and strengthen it, that imprison, draw along, fasten, are pervasive; and the words themselves have the solidity and firmness that make us call them 'real'; they are at the farthest remove from abstraction. Instances of this kind of firm reality are in nearly every line: 'free as the road', 'as large as store', 'harvest but a thorn To let me blood', 'restore ... with cordial fruit', and so on. The 'moral' of the poem doesn't involve any command to insulate oneself from life: the references to fruit, harvest, etc. are the opposite of grudging, and we feel the presence of a sensuous active life in the very quality and character of the words themselves. We feel that when Herbert wrote 'restore' he meant us to receive its full meaning of 're-store'. The line 'Call in thy death's-head there, tie up thy fears' is a fine example of familiar words used for striking effect. Herbert was explicit and downright about his fondness for his native tongue:

> *I like our language, as our men and coast;*
> *Who cannot dress it well, want wit, not words.*

Of course, it is possible for an interest in the 'concrete' to be excessive. There is no good reason, for example, to embrace 'foreword' to the complete exclusion of 'preface'. It was an excess of zeal that led the Dorset poet William Barnes to substitute 'pitches of suchness' for 'degrees of comparison'! There was surely no need to search for a concrete phrase to express a conception that is in its nature abstract.

(Incidentally: the word 'degree' itself contains the meaning of 'step', though it is now to most of us quite an abstract word; in *Twelfth Night*, when Viola says to Olivia 'I pity you', Olivia replies 'That's a degree to love', and Viola retorts 'No, not a grise', meaning 'step'.) Even Hopkins with all his extraordinarily close packing of concrete words, doesn't by any means exclude the abstract: one of his finest poems begins thus:

> *Earnest, earthless, equal, attuneable, vaulty, voluminous, ... stupendous Evening strains to be ...*

But these words really are *used*. The poet is expressing his sense of the gradual, inevitable coming on of evening, a tremendous force enveloping everything, obliterating variety and differences, making everything 'equal', striving to become darkness. Especially when they are read aloud the words seem to rise from the steady opening through a gradually deepening movement and sound to the climax in 'strains'. The words will bear the closest scrutiny for their meaning and will also be found to be richly suggestive: 'voluminous', for instance, has in it both the weighty 'volume' and the impalpable 'luminous'; 'stupendous' has, as well as its strong meaning and sound spreading over into the following line, the suggestion of 'pendulous'. 'Stupendous Evening strains ...' has great physical weight; they are slow, straining words when combined like this. Even the colourless suffixes 'less', 'able', 'ous', help to diffuse a kind of light evenness through the line, counterbalancing the heavier sounds of 'ear', 'vault', etc. Like the single word 'voluminous', the whole line has both a weighty power and an impalpability, and this union suggests the character of the process that is being described. Hopkins's words act as well as state.

With regard to prose, the accepted view or judgement that this suggestive concreteness of diction is not so essential as in poetry, seems on the whole indisputable. Especially in longer pieces of prose writing, where significances are gradually built up, and where the final effect, or effects, depend on the accumulation and coming together of the different elements, a continuous, packed concreteness would, obviously, be out of place. In a good novel, for instance, there will usually be some sort of alternation, which would be found illuminating in a full appraisal of the experience given in the novel, between the more direct-impact kind of writing and the reflective and commentative kind; the more highly-charged passages will have, in general, the more concrete diction.

There is no question of any law in this matter of diction, no 'rule' as to what is right and proper, in prose any more than in poetry. L. H. Myers's way of using language is different from the way we usually associate with James Joyce: Joyce characteristically crowds sensuous words together, aiming at the effects of poetry; Myers is more discursive, less concentrated, more like what we ordinarily call prosaic as opposed to poetic. Both ways are valid; both *Ulysses* and *The Root and the Flower* are extremely valuable novels. Similarly, Henry James is less 'concrete' than D. H. Lawrence; both are great writers. These comparisons are given here, perhaps superflously, to indicate that it is not just the degree of concreteness in language that makes for excellence; a sequence of the most 'physical' words is quite ineffective if they are not organized by the writer for worth-while ends. But it should also be borne in mind that our comparisons are between literary artists, and not between literary artists and other kinds of writer – historian, geologist, economist, etc. The language of both James and Myers often makes itself 'felt'.

It seems probable that there is little deep or lasting satisfaction for most readers in the kind of writing where words are used only as perfunctory symbols for things and as vehicles for ideas and information; that is to say, where the words have been used without a sense of their active power and of their roots in the soil of living activities and perceptions and so in the accents of the living speech that is intimately connected with such activities. The greater the mastery of language that a writer has, feeling the particular, precise force and nuance of the words he uses, the more fully and finely he can convey his sense of life, his experience of 'felt life', whether he is describing a bird's flight or recording his deep and wide awareness of some human situation, some pattern of human relationships.

Hopkins was an accomplished scholar; but though his Greek and Latin unquestionably helped him to his great understanding of the potentialities of words, his poetry is English poetry. Strange as it is to the newcomer, it is nevertheless based firmly on the words, the accent, the movement, of the spoken language. It is because of this that Hopkins has been so frequently invoked in the course of this section; for his poetry illustrates a way of using language that has tended to be superseded since the seventeenth century (with some notable exceptions) by a less 'rooted' way. Hopkins's kestrel hawk in the morning air,

> *... then off, off forth on swing,*
> *As a skate's heel sweeps smooth on a bow-bend: the hurl and gliding*
> *Rebuffed the big wind ...*

is no

> *Light inhabitant of ethereal realms*
> *Where Jove and all his satellites disport.*

It is a bird that he has seen, watched, appreciated with both a keen eye and a keen exhilaration, and he describes it in words that are buoyant, supple, and yet firm.

PASSAGES FOR CRITICISM

THE passages that follow are intended for appreciation and comparison in pairs. A preference may be stated if one passage is felt to be a better piece of writing than the other. Although some of the passages have been chosen primarily for illustration of a particular point – e.g. imagery in No. 6 – criticism in all cases should be as comprehensive as possible.

It may be useful here to touch upon, in the form of questions that the reader may ask himself to aid analysis, some of the points discussed in the several sections. The order in which the questions are given has no significance; and all, of course, are not applicable in the same degree to all the passages. They are important questions; but they are in some cases too 'wide' to be of a more than limited usefulness. They should be used only as a suggestive basis, and in every case where statements are made arising out of a consideration of them, support for the statement should be supplied by instancing the relevant point or detail in the writing that is being examined:

Are (is) the sound and movement really expressive? does it help to convey the experience that the writer is aiming at? does it positively function? or is the rhythm of the over-mechanical kind? too insistent? or flat? the sound too much in isolation from or even at variance with the 'meaning'?

What is the character of the diction? is it predominantly of the 'felt' kind, 'concrete', perhaps strongly 'physical'? unaffected? homely? stilted? over-literary? is it perhaps adopted by the author to serve a particular end? (as an orator, for example, adopts an 'impressive' manner and diction).

Is the theme 'naturally' developed? or is there a lack of 'inevitability', a sense of artificial arrangement?

Is the feeling true? simple? complex? given a particular presentation? undisciplined and excessive? crude? vague? stale?

Does the imagery help to illuminate, to enrich? is it apt? has it enriching associations? is it 'worked' for merely striking effect? simple and good? simple and bad? concise and vivid? diffuse? concentrating or leading away the attention?

Is the writer's 'thought' more than, a richer process than, abstract reasoning or reflexion? are his senses engaged in it? is it 'individual', with (perhaps) some emotional significance for the writer? or is it of the more general ratiocinative kind?

Does the writer seem to force himself unduly on our attention? is he too loud? perhaps over-confident and blustering? or genuinely vigorous? quiet? detached? affectedly over-solemn? unaffectedly serious?

Do his 'devices' really function? really 'belong' to and enhance the total effect? or are they clever (or obvious) embellishments?

There are, of course, many ramifications of the questions, beyond the simple alternatives offered in some of them. And 'yes' and 'no' answers are, obviously, inadequate: literary criticism is not a science. Our analyses and questions are to help us to know just what it is we are reading, and ultimately that we should enjoy and profit more from our reading. Matthew Arnold may fittingly have the last word: 'It is the critic's first duty – prior even to his duty of stigmatizing the bad – to welcome everything that is good.'

1 (a)   *To Daffodils*

> Fair daffodils, we weep to see
>   You haste away so soon;
> As yet the early-rising sun
>   Has not attain'd his noon.
>   Stay, stay
>   Until the hasting day
>   Has run
>   But to the evensong;
> And having pray'd together, we
>   Will go with you along.

We have short time to stay, as you,
　　We have as short a spring;
As quick a growth to meet decay,
　　As you, or anything.
　　　　We die
　　As your hours do, and dry
　　　　Away
　　Like to the summer's rain;
Or as the pearls of morning's dew,
　　Ne'er to be found again.

ROBERT HERRICK

(b)　　　　　　　　　*Life*

I made a posy while the day ran by:
Here will I smell my remnant out, and tie
　　My life within this band;
But time did beckon to the flowers, and they
By noon most cunningly did steal away,
　　And wither'd in my hand.

My hand was next to them, and then my heart;
I took, without more thinking, in good part
　　Time's gentle admonition;
Who did so sweetly Death's sad taste convey,
　　Yet surging the suspicion.

Farewell, dear flowers; sweetly your time ye spent,
Fit while ye lived for smell or ornament,
　　And after death for cures.
I follow straight, without complaints or grief;
Since if my scent be good, I care not if
　　It be as short as yours.

GEORGE HERBERT

2 (a)　　　　　　From *Modern Painters*

Such precipices are among the most impressive as well as
the most really dangerous of mountain ranges; in many
spots inaccessible with safety either from below or from
above; dark in colour, robed with everlasting mourning,

for ever tottering like a great fortress shaken by war, fearful
as much in their weakness as in their strength, and yet
gathered after every fall into darker frowns and unhumilia-
ted threatening; for ever incapable of comfort or of healing
from herb or flower, nourishing no root in their crevices,
touched by no hue of life on buttress or ledge, but, to the
utmost, desolate; knowing no shaking of leaves in the wind,
nor of grass beside the stream, – no motion but their own
mortal shivering, the dreadful crumbling of atom from atom
in their corrupting stones; knowing no sound of living
voice or living tread, cheered neither by the kid's bleat nor
the marmot's cry; haunted only by uninterrupted echoes
from far off, wandering hither and thither, among their
walls, unable to escape, and by the hiss of angry torrents,
and sometimes the shriek of a bird that flits near the face
of them, and sweeps frightened back from under their
shadow into the gulph of air; and, sometimes, when the echo
has fainted, and the wind has carried the sound of the torrent away, and the bird has vanished, and the mouldering
stones are still for a little time, – a brown moth, opening
and shutting its wings upon a grain of dust, may be the only
thing that moves, or feels, in all the waste of weary precipice
darkening five thousand feet of the blue depth of heaven.

JOHN RUSKIN

(b)   From *The Captain's Doll*

He had come to a rift in the ice. He sat near the edge and
looked down. Clean, pure ice, fused with pale colour, and
fused into intense copper-sulphate blue away down in the
crack. It was not like crystal, but fused as one fuses a borax
bead under a blow-flame. And keenly, wickedly blue in the
depths of the crack.

He looked upwards. He had not half mounted the slope.
So on he went, upon the huge body of the soft-fleshed ice,
slanting his way sometimes on all fours, sometimes using his
coat, usually hitting-in with the side of his heel. Hannele
down below was crying him to come back. But two other
youths were now almost level with him.

So he struggled on till he was more or less over the brim. There he stood and looked at the ice. It came down from above in a great hollow world of ice. A world, a terrible place of hills and valleys and slopes, all motionless, all of ice. Away above the grey mist-cloud was looming bigger. And near at hand were long huge cracks, side by side, like gills in the ice. It would seem as if the ice breathed through these great ridged gills. One could look down into the series of gulfs, fearful depths, and the colour burning that acid, intense blue, intenser as the crack went deeper. And the crests of the open gills ridged and grouped pale blue above the crevices. It seemed as if the ice breathed there.

The wonder, the terror, and the bitterness of it. Never a warm leaf to unfold, never a gesture of life to give off. A world sufficient unto itself in lifelessness, all this ice.

He turned to go down, though the youths were passing beyond him. And seeing the naked translucent ice heaving downwards in a vicious curve, always the same dark translucency underfoot, he was afraid. If he slipped, he would certainly slither the whole way down, and break some of his bones. Even when he sat down, he had to cling with his finger-nails in the ice, because if he had started to slide he would have slid the whole way down on his trouser-seat, precipitously, and have landed heaven knows how.

D. H. LAWRENCE

3 (a)   From *The Prelude*

                                        . . . Ere I had told
Ten birth-days, when among the mountain slopes
Frost, and the breath of frosty wind, had snapped
The last autumnal crocus, 'twas my joy
With store of springes o'er my shoulder hung
To range the open heights where woodcocks run
Along the smooth green turf. Through half the night,
Scudding away from snare to snare, I plied
That anxious visitation; – moon and stars
Were shining o'er my head. I was alone,

And seemed to be a trouble to the peace
That dwelt among them. Sometimes it befell
In these night wanderings, that a strong desire
O'erpowered my better reason, and the bird
Which was the captive of another's toil
Became my prey; and when the deed was done
I heard among the solitary hills
Low breathings coming after me, and sounds
Of undistinguishable motion, steps
Almost as silent as the turf they trod.

WILLIAM WORDSWORTH

(b) *September 1819*

The sylvan slopes with corn-clad fields
Are hung, as if with golden shields,
Bright trophies of the sun!
Like a fair sister of the sky,
Unruffled doth the blue lake lie,
The mountains looking on.

And, sooth to say, yon vocal grove,
Albeit uninspired by love,
By love untaught to ring,
May well afford to mortal ear
An impulse more profoundly dear
Than music of the Spring.

For *that* from turbulence and heat
Proceeds, from some uneasy seat
In nature's struggling frame,
Some region of impatient life:
And jealousy, and quivering strife,
Therein a portion claim.

This, this is holy; – while I hear
These vespers of another year,
This hymn of thanks and praise,
My spirits seem to mount above
The anxieties of human love,
And earth's precarious days.

But list! – though winter storms be nigh,
Unchecked is that sweet harmony:
There lives Who can provide
For all his creatures; and in Him
Even like the radiant Seraphim,
Those choristers confide.

WILLIAM WORDSWORTH

4 (a)   From *The Ordeal of Richard Feveral*

Away with Systems! Away with a corrupt World! Let us breathe the air of the Enchanted Island.

Golden lie the meadows: golden run the streams; red gold is on the pine-stems. The sun is coming down to earth, and walks the fields and the waters.

The sun is coming down to earth, and the fields and the waters shout to him golden shouts. He comes, and his heralds run before him, and touch the leaves of oaks and planes and beeches lucid green, and the pine-stems redder gold; leaving brightest footprints upon thickly-weeded banks, where the foxglove's last upper-bells incline and bramble-shoots wander amid moist rich herbage. The plumes of the woodland are alight; and beyond them, over the open, 'tis a race with a long-thrown shadows; a race across the heaths and up the hills, till, at the farthest bourne of mounted eastern cloud, the heralds of the sun lay rosy fingers and rest.

Sweet are the shy recesses of the woodland. The ray treads softly there. A film athwart the pathway quivers many-hued against purple shade fragrant with warm pines, deep moss-beds, feathery ferns. The little brown squirrel drops tail, and leaps; the inmost bird is startled to a chance tuneless note. From silence into silence things move.

Peeps of the revelling splendour above and around enliven the conscious full heart within. The flaming West, the crimson heights, shower their glories through volu-minous leafage. But these are bowers where deep bliss dwells, imperial joy, that owes no fealty to yonder glories, in which the young lamb gambols and the spirits of men are glad. Descend, great Radiance! embrace creation with beneficent fire, and pass from us! You and the vice-regal light that succeeds to you, and all heavenly pageants, are the ministers and the slaves of the throbbing content within.

For this is the home of the enchantment. . . .

GEORGE MEREDITH

(b)   From *The Life of the Fields*

Here was the spring, at the foot of the perpendicular rock, moss-grown low down, and overrun with creeping ivy higher. Green thorn bushes filled the chinks and made a wall to the well, and the long narrow hart's-tongue streaked the face of the cliff. Behind, the thick thorns hid the source of the streamlet, in front rose the solid rock, upon the right side the sward came to the edge – it shook every now and then as the horses in the shade of the elms stamped their feet – on the left hand the ears of wheat peered over the verge. A rocky cell in concentrated silence of green things. Now and again a finch, a starling, or a sparrow would come meaning to drink – athirst from the meadow or the corn-field – and start and almost entangle their wings in the bushes, so completely astonished that anyone should be there. The spring rises in a hollow under the rock imperceptibly, and without bubble or sound. The fine sand of the shallow basin is undisturbed! – no tiny water-volcano pushes up a dome of particles. Nor is there any crevice in the stone, but the basin is always full and always running over. As it slips from the brim a gleam of sunshine falls through the boughs and meets it. To this cell I used to come once now and then on a summer's day, tempted, perhaps, like the finches, by the sweet cool water, but drawn also by a feeling that could not be analysed. Stooping, I lifted the water in the hollow of my hand – carefully, lest the sand might be disturbed – and the sunlight gleamed on it as it slipped through my fingers. Alone in the green-roofed cave, alone with the sunlight and the pure water, there was a sense of something more than these. The water was more to me than water, and the sun than sun. The gleaming rays

on the water in my palm held me for a moment, the touch
of the water gave me something from itself. A moment, and
the gleam was gone, the water flowing away, but I had had
them. Beside the physical water and physical light I had
received from them their beauty; they had communicated
to me this silent mystery. The pure and beautiful water,
the pure, clear, and beautiful light, each had given me
something of their truth.

So many times I came to it, toiling up the long and
shadowless hill in the burning sunshine, often carrying a
vessel to take some of it home with me. There was a brook,
indeed; but this was different, it was the spring; it was taken
home as a beautiful flower might be brought. It is not the
physical water, it is the sense or feeling that it conveys. Nor
is it the physical sunshine; it is the sense of inexpressible
beauty which it brings with it. Of such I still drink, and hope
to do so still deeper.

RICHARD JEFFERIES

5 (a)   From *Paradise Lost*

                    Him the Almighty Power
Hurled headlong flaming from the ethereal sky,
With hideous ruin and combustion, down
To bottomless perdition, there to dwell
In adamantine chains and penal fire,
Who durst defy the Omnipotent to arms.
   Nine times the space that measures day and night
To mortal men, he, with his horrid crew,
Lay vanquished, rolling in the fiery gulf,
Confounded, though immortal. But his doom
Reserved him to more wrath; for now the thought
Both of lost happiness and lasting pain
Torments him: round he throws his baleful eyes,
That witnessed huge affliction and dismay,
Mixed with obdurate pride and steadfast hate.
At once, as far as Angel's ken, he views
The dismal situation waste and wild.
A dungeon horrible, on all sides round,

As one great furnace flamed; yet from those flames
No light; but rather darkness visible
Served only to discover sights of woe,
Regions of sorrow, doleful shades, where peace
And rest can never dwell, hope never comes
That comes to all, but torture without end
Still urges, and a fiery deluge, fed
With ever-burning sulphur unconsumed.

(b)   From *Paradise Lost*

When I behold this goodly frame, this World,
Of Heaven and Earth consisting and compute
Their magnitudes – this Earth, a spot, a grain,
An atom, with the Firmament compared
And all her number'd stars, that seem to roll
Spaces incomprehensible (for such
Their distance argues, and their swift return
Diurnal) merely to officiate light
Round this opacous Earth, this punctual spot,
One day and night, in all their vast survey
Useless besides – reasoning, I oft admire
How Nature, wise and frugal, could commit
Such disproportions, with superflous hand
So many noble bodies to create,
Greater, so manifold, to this one use,
For aught appears, and on their Orbs impose
Such restless revolution day by day
Repeated, while the sedentary Earth,
That better might with far less compass move,
Served by more noble than herself, attains
Her end without least motion, and receives,
As tribute, such a sumless journey brought
Of incorporeal speed, her warmth and light:
Speed, to describe whose swiftness number fails.

                                        JOHN MILTON

6 (a)   From *Richard II*

(The Duchess of Gloucester is lamenting the death of her
husband to John of Gaunt, his brother, and trying to incite
him to avenge it.)

> Finds brotherhood in thee no sharper spur?
> Hath love in thy old blood no living fire?
> Edward's seven sons, whereof thyself art one,
> Were as seven vials of his sacred blood,
> Or seven fair branches springing from one root:
> Some of those seven are dried by nature's course,
> Some of those branches by the Destinies cut;
> But Thomas, my dear lord, my life, my Gloster,
> One vial full of Edward's sacred blood,
> One flourishing branch of his most royal root,
> Is crackt, and all the precious liquor split,
> Is hackt down and his summer-leaves all faded,
> By envy's hand and murder's bloody axe.

WILLIAM SHAKESPEARE

(b)   From *King Lear*

(Cornwall has asked Kent, who has just had an encounter
with the obsequious servingman Oswald, why he is angry.
Kent replies.)

That such a slave as this should wear a sword,
Who wears no honesty. Such smiling rogues as these
Like rats, oft bite the holy cords a-twain
Which are too intrinse t'unloose; smooth every passion
That in the natures of their lords rebel,
Bring oil to fire, snow to their colder moods;
Renege, affirm and turn their halcyon beaks
With every gale and vary of their masters,
Knowing nought, like dogs, but following. –
A plague upon your epileptic visage!
Smile you my speeches, as I were a fool?
Goose, if I had you upon Sarum plain,
I'ld drive ye cackling home to Camelot.

WILLIAM SHAKESPEARE

7 (a)   From *The French Revolution*

It is yellow July evening, we say, the thirteenth of the
month; eve of the Bastille day, – when 'M. Marat', four
years ago, in the crowd of the Pont Neuf, shrewdly required
of that Besenval Hussar-party, which had such friendly
dispositions, 'to dismount, and give up their arms, then';
and became notable among Patriot men. Four years: what
a road he has travelled; – and sits now, about half past
seven of the clock, stewing in slipper bath; sore afflicted; ill
of Revolutionary Fever, – of what other malady this History
had rather not name. Excessively sick and worn, poor man:
with precisely eleven-pence-halfpenny of ready money, in
paper; with slipper-bath; strong three-footed stool for
writing on, the while; and a squalid – Washerwoman, one
may call her: that is his civic establishment in Medical-
School Street; thither and not elsewhither has his road led
him. Not to the reign of Brotherhood and Perfect Felicity;
yet surely on the way towards that? – Hark, a rap again!
A musical woman's voice, refusing to be rejected; it is the
Citoyenne who would do France a service. Marat, recog-
nizing from within, cries, Admit her. Charlotte Corday is
admitted.

Citoyen Marat, I am from Caen the seat of rebellion, and
wished to speak with you. – Be seated, *mon enfant*. Now what
are the Traitors doing at Caen? What Deputies are at
Caen? – Charlotte names some Deputies. 'Their heads
shall fall within a fortnight,' croaks the eager people's-
friend, clutching his tablets to write: *Barbaroux, Pétion*,
writes he with bare shrunk arm, turning aside in the bath:
Pétion, and *Louvet*, and – Charlotte has drawn her knife from
the sheath; plunges it, with one sure stroke into the writer's
heart. '*À moi, chère amie*, Help, dear!' no more could the
Death-choked say or shriek. The helpful Washerwoman
running in, there is no Friend of the People, or Friend of the
Washerwoman left; but this life with a groan gushes out,
indignant, to the shades below.

                                        THOMAS CARLYLE

(b)   From *A Cypresse Grove*

If on the great theatre of this earth, amongst the numberless
number of men, to die were only proper to thee and thine,
then, undoubtedly, thou hadst reason to grudge at so severe
and partial a law. But since it is a necessity, from which
never an age by-past hath been exempted, and unto which
these which be, and so many as are to come, are thralled
(no consequent of life being more common and familiar),
why shouldst thou, with unprofitable and nothing-availing
stubbornness, oppose to so inevitable and necessary a
condition? This is the highway of mortality, our general
home: behold what millions have trod it before thee! what
multitudes shall after thee, with them which at that same
instant run! In so universal a calamity (if death be one),
private complaints cannot be heard: with so many royal
palaces, it is small loss to see thy poor cabin burn. Shall the
heavens stay their ever-rolling wheels (for what is the motion
of them but the motion of a swift and ever-whirling wheel,
which twinneth forth, and again upwindeth our life), and
hold still time to prolong thy miserable days, as if the highest
of their working were to do homage unto thee? Thy death
is a piece of the order of this *All*, a part of the life of this
world; for while the world is the world, some creatures must
die, and others take life. Eternal things are raised far above
this orb of generation and corruption, where the first matter
like a still flowing and ebbing sea, with diverse waves, but
the same water, keepeth a restless and never tiring current;
what is below, in the universality of the kind, not in itself
doth abide: man a long line of years hath continued, this
man every hundred is swept away.

                                           W. DRUMMOND

8 (a)   From *Despondency*

Oppress'd with grief, oppress'd with care,
A burden more than I can bear,
I set me down and sigh:
O life! thou art a galling load,
Along a rough, a weary road,

To wretches such as I!
Dim-backward as I cast my view,
What sick'ning scenes appear!
What sorrows yet may pierce me thro',
Too justly I may fear!
Still caring, despairing,
Must be my bitter doom;
My woes here shall close ne'er,
But with the closing tomb!

ROBERT BURNS

(b)   *The Banks o' Doon*

Ye flowery banks o' bonnie Doon,
How can ye blume sae fair!
How can ye chant, ye little birds,
And I sae fu' o' care.

Thou'll break my heart, thou bonnie bird,
That sings upon the bough;
Thou minds me o' the happy days,
When my fause love was true.

Thou'll break my heart, thou bonnie bird,
That sings beside thy mate;
For sae I sat, and sae I sang,
And wist na o' my fate.

Aft hae I rov'd by bonnie Doon,
To see the wood-bine twine,
And ilka bird sang o' its love,
And sae did I o' mine.

Wi' lightsome heart I pu'd a rose
Frae off its thorny tree;
And my fause luver staw the rose,
But left the thorn wi' me.

ROBERT BURNS

9 (a)   *The Immortals*

I killed them, but they would not die.
Yea! all the day and all the night
For them I could not rest nor sleep,
Nor guard from them nor hide in flight.

Then in my agony I turned
And made my hands red in their gore.
In vain – for faster than I slew
They rose more cruel than before.

I killed and killed with slaughter mad;
I killed till all my strength was gone.
And still they rose to torture me,
For Devils only die for fun.

I used to think the Devil hid
In women's smiles and wine's carouse.
I called him Satan, Balzebub.
But now I call him dirty louse.

ISAAC ROSENBERG

(b)   *Louse Hunting*

Nudes – stark and glistening,
Yelling in lurid glee. Grinning faces
And raging limbs
Whirl over the floor one fire.
For a shirt verminously busy
Yon soldier tore from his throat, with oaths
Godhead might shrink at, but not the lice.
And soon the shirt was aflare
Over the candle he'd lit while we lay.

Then we all sprang up and stript
To hunt the verminous brood.
Soon like a demons' pantomime
The place was raging.
See the silhouettes agape,
See the gibbering shadows
Mixed with the battled arms on the wall.

See gargantuan hooked fingers
Pluck in supreme flesh
To smutch supreme littleness.
See the merry limbs in hot Highland fling
Because some wizard vermin
Charmed from the quiet this revel
When our ears were half lulled
By the dark music
Blown from Sleep's trumpet.

ISAAC ROSENBERG

10 (a)   From *The Newcomes*

Boulogne was their present abiding place – refuge of how
many thousands of other unfortunate Britons – and to this
friendly port I betook myself speedily, having the address
of Colonel Newcome. His quarters were in a quiet grass-
grown old street of the Old Town. None of the family were
at home when I called. There was indeed no servant to
answer the bell, but the good-natured French domestic of
a neighbouring lodger told me that the young Monsieur
went out every day to make his designs, and that I should
probably find the elder gentleman upon the rampart, where
he was in the custom of going every day. I strolled along by
those pretty old walks and bastions, under the pleasant
trees which shadow them, and the grey old gabled houses
from which you look down upon the gay new city, and the
busy port, and the piers stretching into the shining sea
dotted with a hundred white sails or black smoking steam-
ers, and bounded by the friendly lines of the bright English
shore. There are few prospects more charming than the
familiar view from those old French walls – few places where
young children may play, and ruminating old age repose,
more pleasantly than on those peaceful rampart gardens.

I found our dear old friend seated on one of the benches,
a newspaper on his knees, and by his side a red-cheeked
little French lass, upon whose lap Thomas Newcome the
younger lay sleeping. The Colonel's face flushed up when
he saw me. As he advanced a step or two towards me, I
could see that he trembled in his walk. His hair had grown

almost quite white. He looked now to be more than his age
– he whose carriage last year had been so erect, whose figure
had been so straight and manly. I was very much moved at
meeting him, and at seeing the sad traces which pain and
grief had left in the countenance of the dear old man.

'So you are come to see me, my good young friend,' cried
the Colonel with a trembling voice. 'It is very, very kind
of you. Is not this a pretty drawing-room to receive our
friends in? we have not many of them now. Boy and I come
and sit here for hours every day. Hasn't he grown a fine
boy? He can say several words now, sir, and can walk
surprisingly well. Soon he will be able to walk with his
grandfather, and then Marie will not have the trouble to
wait upon either of us.' He repeated this sentiment in his
pretty old French, and turning with a bow to Marie. The
girl said Monsieur knew very well that she did not desire
better than to come out with baby; that it was better than
staying at home, *pardieu*; and, the clock striking at this
moment, she rose up with her child, crying out that it was
time to return, or Madame would scold.

'Mrs Mackenzie has rather a short temper,' the Colonel
said, with a gentle smile. 'Poor thing, she has had a great
deal to bear in consequence, Pen, of my imprudence. I am
glad you never took shares in our bank. I should not be so
glad to see you as I am now, if I had brought losses upon
you as I have upon so many of my friends.' I, for my part,
trembled to hear that the good old man was under the
domination of the Campaigner.

W. M. THACKERAY

(b)   From *Middlemarch*

(Bulstrode, the respectable banker, is in great fear lest
Raffles, an old acquaintance of his, should divulge certain
facts about his earlier life. Raffles is now ill at a house
Bulstrode has recently bought. The previous day to this,
Bulstrode has refused the request of Lydgate, a young
doctor in financial trouble, for a loan of a thousand pounds.)

It was nearly the middle of the day before Lydgate
arrived: he had meant to come earlier, but had been

detained he said; and his shattered looks were noticed by
Bulstrode. But he immediately threw himself into the consideration of the patient, and inquired strictly into all that
had occurred. Raffles was worse, would take hardly any
food, was persistently wakeful and restlessly raving; but
still not violent. Contrary to Bulstrode's alarmed expectation, he took little notice of Lydgate's presence, and continued to talk or murmur incoherently.

'What do you think of him?' said Bulstrode, in private.

'The symptoms are worse.'

'You are less hopeful?'

'No; I still think he may come round. Are you going to
stay here yourself?' said Lydgate, looking at Bulstrode with
an abrupt question, which made him uneasy, though in
reality it was not due to any suspicious conjecture.

'Yes, I think so,' said Bulstrode, governing himself and
speaking with deliberation. 'Mrs Bulstrode is advised of the
reasons which detain me. Mrs Abel and her husband are
not experienced enough to be left quite alone, and this kind
of responsibility is scarcely included in their service of me.
You have some fresh instructions, I presume.'

The chief new instruction that Lydgate had to give was
on the administration of extremely moderate doses of
opium, in case of the sleeplessness continuing after several
hours. He had taken the precaution of bringing opium in
his pocket, and he gave minute directions to Bulstrode as to
the doses, and the point at which they should cease. He insisted on the risk of not ceasing; and repeated his order
that no alcohol should be given.

'From what I see of the case,' he ended, 'narcotism is the
only thing I should be much afraid of. He may wear through
even without much food. There's a good deal of strength
in him.'

'You look ill yourself, Mr Lydgate – a most unusual, I
may say unprecedented thing in my knowledge of you,'
said Bulstrode, showing a solicitude as unlike his indifference
the day before, as his present recklessness about his own
fatigue was unlike his habitual self-cherishing anxiety. 'I
fear you are harassed.'

'Yes, I am,' said Lydgate, brusquely, holding his hat, and ready to go.

'Something new, I fear,' said Bulstrode, inquiringly. 'Pray be seated.'

'No, thank you,' said Lydgate, with some *hauteur*. 'I mentioned to you yesterday what was the state of my affairs. There is nothing to add, except that the execution has since then been actually put into my house. One can tell a good deal of trouble in a short sentence. I will say good-morning.'

'Stay, Mr Lydgate, stay,' said Bulstrode; 'I have been reconsidering this subject. I was yesterday taken by surprise, and saw it superficially. Mrs Bulstrode is anxious for her niece, and I myself should grieve at a calamitous change in your position. Claims on me are numerous, but on reconsideration, I esteem it right that I should incur a small sacrifice rather than leave you unaided. You said, I think, that a thousand pounds would suffice entirely to free you from your burthens, and enable you to recover a firm stand?'

'Yes,' said Lydgate, a great leap of joy within him surmounting every other feeling; 'that would pay all my debts and leave me a little on hand. I could set about economizing in our way of living. And by-and-by my practice might look up.'

'If you will wait a moment, Mr Lydgate, I will draw a cheque to that amount. I am aware that help, to be effectual in these cases, must be thorough.'

While Bulstrode wrote, Lydgate turned to the window thinking of his home – thinking of his life with its good start saved from frustration, its good purpose still unbroken.

'You can give me a note of hand for this, Mr Lydgate,' said the banker, advancing towards him with the cheque. 'And by-and-by, I hope, you may be in circumstances gradually to repay me. Meanwhile, I have pleasure in thinking that you will be released from further difficulty.'

'I am deeply obliged to you,' said Lydgate. 'You have restored to me the prospect of working with some happiness and some chance of good.'

GEORGE ELIOT

BOOK LIST

THE slight doubt that one usually feels when suggesting a book list on any given subject is perhaps mainly due to two things: one, that no list of books can ever be reckoned complete and final; and two, that some of the books suggested are probably more consistently excellent than others. Another thing that helps to make one discreet about claims to comprehensiveness is the knowledge that we may often alight on pieces of helpful criticism in writing that is not specifically 'critical'. For instance, there are to be found some most illuminating remarks on rhythm and rhyming and feeling in some of D. H. Lawrence's letters (e.g. on pages 133, 151 and 152, 153–6, 307–8: Heinemann, 1934); there are T. S. Eliot's accounts in 'Four Quartets' of his long struggle to use words with their full force and effectiveness; and in the good work of good novelists, say George Eliot or Henry James, we are at any time likely to encounter some remark or some description of an incident or gesture which reveals the author's insight into the relation of thought and feeling and the relation of both to language.

The following books will be found invaluable for the wealth of literary criticism which they provide:

Essays in Criticism	Matthew Arnold
The Problem of Style	Middleton Murry
Aspects of Literature	Middleton Murry
Countries of the Mind (1 and 2)	Middleton Murry
Selected Essays	T. S. Eliot
*New Bearings in English Poetry	F. R. Leavis
*Revaluation	F. R. Leavis
Determinations	F. R. Leavis (editor)
Approach to Shakespeare	D. A. Traversi
Reading and Discrimination	Denys Thompson
*The Great Tradition	F. R. Leavis
The Principles of Literary Criticism	I. A. Richards
Practical Criticism	I. A. Richards
Seven Types of Ambiguity	William Empson
*Explorations	L. C. Knights
*The Common Pursuit	F. R. Leavis

* Published by Penguins.

INDEX